The EIS Book

Information Systems for Top Managers

by
Alan Paller

with
Richard Laska

Dow Jones-Irwin
Homewood, IL 60430

This publication is designed to provide accurate and
authoritative information in regard to the subject matter
covered. It is sold with the understanding that the
publisher is not engaged in rendering legal, accounting, or
other professional service. If legal advice or other expert
assistance is required, the services of a competent
professional person should be sought.

*From a Declaration of Principles jointly adopted by a Committee
of the American Bar Association and a Committee of Publishers.*

Library of Congress Cataloging-in-Publication Data

Paller, Alan.
   The EIS book : information systems for top managers / Alan Paller,
Richard Laska.
     p.   cm.
   ISBN 1-55623-244-6
   1. Management— Data processing.   2. Decision support system.
3. Executives.   4. Management information systems.   I. Laska,
Richard. II. Title.
HD30.2.P355   1990
658.4′038—dc20   89–29819
                                                    CIP

Printed in the United States of America
1 2 3 4 5 6 7 8 9 DO 6 5 4 3 2 1 0 9

Dedication

This book is dedicated to James Webb, a true teacher,
for the insight and wisdom of his stories, and to
Dr. Pat Tokarz, a saver of lives.

Acknowledgements

We want to thank the many reviewers
whose comments and corrections added immeasurably
to the value of this book. We would like to list you by
name, but appreciate the need for anonymity.
Suffice it to say that we know who you are, and
we thank you.

Thanks also goes to all of you who supplied
high-quality EIS displays. We wish we could use them all.
Most of the data in displays used in this book
was modified sufficiently to protect
sensitive information.

Finally, we want to acknowledge a problem with sex.
Throughout the drafts of this book we tested
four approaches to avoid the apparent sexism of
referring to the indefinite third person as *he*.
None worked well enough, so we used the fallback
masculine gender throughout.
No offense meant.

The Authors

The text in this book was designed on a Macintosh II using a Cornerstone display and Pagemaker software. The book is set in Adobe's ITC New Baskerville and Optima typefaces. Graphics were designed using the Adobe Illustrator 88 program. —R. Laska

Contents

1 Why an EIS?
It's Elemental, My Dear

The elemental management *needs* for information and control are constant. Humans long have struggled to perfect the art of executive information transfer. While the need continues, over time, both *what* weconvey and *how* we convey it have changed.

The problems may seem new to us, but they are as old as society itself. A million years ago, the chief executive officer (CEO) of a ragtag band of hunter-gatherers roaming the African veldt needed to invent the major components of an executive information system. Far-fetched? Let's observe our hirsute CEO as he organizes his band for the hunt.

What are the key information and communications problems faced by our furry forbear?

Management: Who's giving the orders?

Control: How do we get the others to follow orders?

Situation: What's our status? How long do we have?

Objective: Where are we going?

Procedures: How do we get there from here?

Relationships: How do we adjust for different hunting skills?

Morale: How do we reward the best hunters and enjoy the trek?

Intelligence: Where's the herd? Are some animals weak and more vulnerable than the rest?

How does Mr. H. Erectus cope? By imaginatively using the latest technologies available—hand signals and grunts.

Things haven't changed much. Grunting and gesturing are still an important part of many executives' repertoires, especially during the rush-hour commute. To these skills, modern executive information systems (EIS) add a very flexible set of management tools.

EIS is not an entirely new phenomenon. Under different guises, true computer terminal-based executive information systems have been available to a select few for two decades. Paper-based executive information systems existed even earlier.

Executive information systems is just the latest, and perhaps not even the best, name for this phenomenon. Decision support systems (DSS) or management information systems (MIS) might be better terms, but these have been usurped by academicians, in one case, and data processing professionals, in the other. Senior management is left scowling in the middle.

Whatever you call it, senior management needed something. Many were frustrated—angry—that so much money was being spent on information systems equipment and people without making the information any more useful to them. It was as though the more they spent, the bigger the pile of paper they had to go through in order to find the information they needed.

The modern EIS was born out of a demand by senior executives for information systems that respond to the real needs of real executives. In some cases, executives created their own staffs and their own information systems.

What these systems are called doesn't really matter. What does matter is what they can do. John Rockart and David DeLong, early pioneers in the field, call them executive support systems. We call them executive information systems. You may call them anything you choose.

In essence, executive information systems are computer-based *information delivery and communications systems* for senior managers. They may bring the latest internal operating information, or Wall Street results, or external news stories, or mail to the desks of senior executives. The same systems also may deliver the same performance information directly to the operations managers.

EIS information is distilled, concentrated down to the most essential facts. At the same time, executive information systems may allow the executive to look beyond these summaries and obtain the finest level of detail about a product, department, or client. As such, EIS systems stand in stark contrast to the piles of printout that most wise executives ignore.

An executive information system has many faces. Personal computers or terminals may dispense EIS information, or the information may be displayed on a large screen projector, or delivered in chartbooks, or pocket card decks for traveling executives.

Why implement an EIS? There are three main benefits: increase profitability or effectiveness, achieve key organizational objectives, and gain a competitive advantage. Not all EIS applications provide all these benefits. Some fail to provide any benefits. But there is no need to fail.

For the executive, an EIS offers the potential to extend knowledge of, and impact upon, both the organization and its competitive environment. For the organization, an EIS can streamline many aspects of the business, allow effective delegation and objective-based management, and save millions . For the EIS director, a successful EIS is a big step up the career ladder.

EIS Successes

When implemented successfully, EIS systems have an extraordinary ability to improve an organization's efficiency, effectiveness, and competitive position. They work because they increase an executive's span of control, save executive time, improve communications, reduce uncertainty, and increase team spirit. In the global competitive environment, most corporations need an EIS to operate effectively.

Phillips Petroleum

The best example is one of the truly great executive information systems in the country–the system developed for Phillips Petroleum. There are several reasons why we consider this a great EIS. The most important is that the people in charge at Phillips credit the EIS with saving them more than $100 million. That's great enough for us.

Late in 1984, corporate raider T. Boone Pickens made a hostile bid for Phillips Petroleum. The corporation's defense was to buy back Pickens's stock. To do this, they had to take on considerable debt and sell off assets. Scarcely a year later, Carl Icahn did the same, and Phillips increased its debt and sold off more assets to buy back his chunk of stock.

The result was that, within two years, the corporation had accumulated an $8.8 billion debt and had been forced to sell off more than $2 billion in assets. Debt soared from 20 to 80 percent of their capital.

If the organization was to survive, Phillips executives had only three options: cut, cut, or cut. So they cut. Management and staff support were reduced by more than one-third. Three distinct layers of management were eliminated. To maintain the business, they left operations staff relatively unscathed. When the dust cleared, they were left with an organization which, if not lo-

botomized, at least had a severe migraine. How to get the information needed to manage? How to manage?

The way Robert Wallace, former president of Phillips 66 Company (part of Phillips Petroleum) described their approach was
simple: Broaden the span of top executive control, put information where the action is, and transfer decision-making authority.
The only way to do this was by implementing a spectacular executive information system. "I didn't want a bunch of staff accumu-
lating new data," recalls Wallace. "I wanted to use the existing
data in the business systems, focus that data at my level, and then
flow it down into the organization on an as-needed basis."

With the expansion of the executive's scope of control, Wallace went from directly managing two senior executives to managing ten. To manage the organization better, it was necessary to
manage information better.

At Phillips, decisions must be made quickly. For example, a
one-cent shift per gallon in the price Phillips charges can mean
millions to the organization. Too high a price and you lose volume. Too low and you give away profit. The EIS was designed to
track, several times per day, the prices, costs, and spot market
price for the petroleum products Phillips bought and sold.

But having the information was not enough. It had to be available to those who could act on it quickly. At Phillips, the best
people to make purchase/sales/price decisions were the firm's
100 managers who worked at the front lines. So the EIS was put
at their service. At the same time, their authority to make decisions autonomously was increased by nearly an order of magnitude. They were being paid for their experience and judgment.
At Phillips, they were also being trusted to exercise that judgment.

As long as all pricing decisions were made centrally, many of
the prices did not reflect local conditions well and were inefficient. The EIS gave local officials the current information to allow them to set prices competitively and profitably. The president and his staff still maintained on-line monitoring of the decisions and the effects those decisions were having. But the authority and information to make those decisions had been transferred down to the people who were closest to the action, who
knew local conditions and competitive position.

"To do all this by conventional means would not have been
possible," Wallace asserts. "The difference between an EIS and a
conventional system is that, with the electronic system, you don't

have to worry about what file the information is buried in. It is available instantaneously—all set up for quick access. The data is real, fluid, and dynamic. That's why it is so meaningful at the executive level."

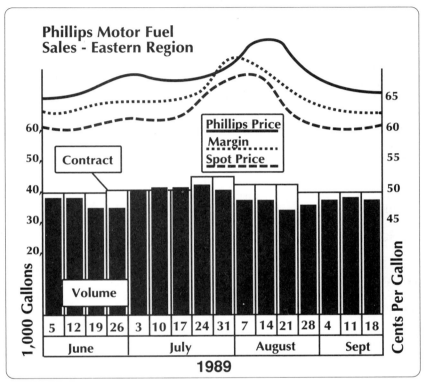

The chart above is an excellent example of the volume of useful, related information that can be packed into one understandable EIS graphic. While the format is from Phillips, the data is, understandably, simulated.

The bottom line? "We got a more profitable operation," notes Wallace, "and that's what we are paid to do. We are also using people more effectively by giving them a greater sense of involvement and participation. No company has greater ability to allow participation and involvement than we do through our EIS." Delegating both information and authority to act allowed people to do their jobs better, and made them feel appreciated by a management who knew what they were doing.

General Electric Corporation

Another successful set of EIS systems was developed for General Electric Corporation (GE). GE has several EIS applications serving engineering, marketing, financial, and general management executives nationwide.

To stay competitive, GE recreated itself by streamlining from seven to five (or less) management layers, and reducing payroll by nearly 100,000 employees while doubling revenue. Most of the middle managers released by GE had been responsible for passing information up and down the management line. Timely operational information and competitive data are essential. It is what allows an organization to adapt rapidly and to meet new challenges. With middle managers going away, GE turned to computers and communications to fill the gap.

As other corporations act to make themselves more competitive, they can be expected to follow Phillips's and GE's lead in reducing layers of management. Consequently, they will be forced to use executive information systems to meet the information needs left unfilled by the departing middle managers.

The Executive Perspective

What information do executives want? To a great extent, it depends upon the individual. Despite the pressures to conform, each executive approaches the job from a slightly different perspective. Executives are people. They show the same range of characteristics, preferences, and prejudices that other people display. Anyone who generalizes about "what executives like" does so knowing that their generalizations will be dead wrong for a large portion of the executive population. With this in mind, we leap into the fray with the following generalizations. We do so in hopes that, imperfect as they may be, they will help technical specialists to understand the executive perspective better.

Of the hundreds of executives we've interviewed in the past two decades, most share the following characteristics.

Executives hate surprises. Even a pleasant surprise reminds the executive that there are important unknowns. The unknown makes executives insecure.

They expect people to listen and act upon what they say. Most successful executives define a few themes for their organization and repeat them at every opportunity. While this usually becomes boring to both the executive and the audience, it is one of the few ways that an executive has of reminding people of the organization's priorities.

They don't like to wait. When they want information, they want it now. Executives do not want information for information's sake—they have some strategy in mind that requires a particular set of data. Executives execute. They make decisions and take actions in an ever-changing environment. If information needed to support today's actions arrives on the executive's desk tomorrow, messenger beware!

They seldom explain the level of detail they need. To them, useful information is like great art—they know it when they see it. This makes the development of an effective EIS as much of an art as it is a science, and requires that the EIS implementor know how to listen, carefully, to the needs of the executive.

They hate to be kept in the dark. To the extent that knowledge is power, lack of good information can be very disarming, especially when a competitor knows more. One of the least pleasant ways of learning what information is expected of you is to have your executive hold you responsible for *not* providing it.

Why Executives Like EIS

Keeping in mind the perspective discussed above, it is easier to understand why executives like EIS. The bottom line, however, is still the bottom line. Executives like EIS systems because they can help commercial organizations to make more money, government agencies to accomplish their missions, and both types of organization to get more out of what they have. With few exceptions, all other motivations for developing an EIS are of secondary importance.

How important is an EIS to their operations? Listen to what one General Motors (GM) executive told *Business Week*:

"We consider our EIS to be so competitive that we will not discuss it in public."

Or ponder what General David Jones, retired chairman of the Joint Chiefs of Staff, said: "EIS is changing the way the military is managed."

Fundamentally, EIS systems help executives in five ways: increase span of control, save time, improve communications, reduce uncertainty, and assist in team-building.

Increase Span of Control

One of the most important functions of an EIS is to help executives implement their initiatives within a multi-layered organization. When someone gains a top management position, the people below believe that individual now has real power. In reality, most top managers are exceedingly frustrated by their lack of ability to get their organizations to act.

We are reminded of a quotation attributed to outgoing President Harry S. Truman. After the election of General Dwight Eisenhower to the presidency in 1952, Truman was not optimistic about Eisenhower's ability to govern. Eisenhower had made his reputation giving orders as supreme allied commander in Europe during World War II. Truman believed that there was an enormous difference between fighting a war in Europe and fighting with a bureaucracy in Washington.

"Poor Ike," Truman lamented, "he'll sit at his cabinet meetings and order that *this* be done and order that *that* be done. Six months later, he'll wonder why nothing happened."

Especially in multi-tiered organizations, intermediate layers of management dilute and deflect so many top management initiatives that few ever are implemented. An EIS can change all that. An effective executive information system makes the senior executive's goals, and the organization's performance, visible. As one EIS pioneer observes, "A terminal on the senior guy's desk is a preemptive strike against middle management. They now know I can see what they are doing."

It is the rare executive who never has said to himself, "Isn't anybody listening?" The flip side of this coin is the old, but true, adage that "what gets watched gets done."

While the idea of management by objective has lost its glitter, it is still the golden rule in the executive suite. Executives who succeed in their jobs set objectives, delegate responsibility, monitor progress, provide support, and exert pressure to make sure the objectives are met. When objectives are met, they reward the people who made it happen.

In short, successful managers are those who manage by objectives. All too often, however, when an executive sets a new objective, the organization does not follow. By keeping the objective in front of the organization at all times, an EIS reinforces the executive's priorities, expands his span of control, and makes things get done.

Save Time

An EIS allows executives to get answers quickly, without spending scarce time of valuable personnel, including their own. Delays in getting information that is essential to making a decision or taking an action mean that the entire issue must be rehashed again, at a later date, when the needed information becomes available. This wastes executive time.

When executives ask a question, people are often pulled off important projects to get an answer for the boss. For example, when Belvin Williams first became Dean at Columbia Teachers College, he was astounded by his organization's reaction to a simple request for information. "Several people spent the better part of a day getting me an answer to one question," Williams recalled.

"When they came back the next day with an answer, and told me how much work it had taken, I was shocked. If they had told me it was going to take that long, I wouldn't have asked fot it. It wasn't worth that much time and effort." Williams's experience is repeated by executives every day. They need information but they don't want to waste staff time getting it.

There are few places where it is more time-consuming for the executive to get information about what is going on than in a large federal agency. In 1976, when Stephen J. Gage took over as assistant administrator of the U. S. Environmental Protection Agency's (EPA) Office of Research and Development, he found an enormous communications gap between top management and bench scientist.

EPA's research office had 1,400 employees either conducting or managing nearly $250 million worth of research projects annually. EPA researchers worked at two dozen locations nationwide, from the Washington, D.C. headquarters to College Station, Alaska and from Duluth, Minnesota to Gulf Breeze, Florida.

The office had a kind of communications gridlock. Headquarters would create annual plans and budgets for the administration and Congress to review and approve. Once approved, the plans and resources were transferred to the field laboratories for implementation. The laboratories, in turn, spent the money with only passing reference to the original plan. Little information on these research projects filtered back to headquarters.

"We couldn't say how many research projects we supported," notes Gage. "I lived in fear that some Congressman would ask me to account for the quarter-billion dollars we spent each year."

To find out what the organization was doing in a particular area required that the executives working in that area quit whatever they were doing and call their field contacts. It not only consumed inordinate time, it also took hours or days to get a decent answer to the simplest inquiry. In response, EPA created an EIS which included project-level information. Within six months, they defined more than 2,600 active research projects. The EIS allowed EPA executives to access project information by any combination of hundreds of parameters from key words, to chemical names, to zip codes.

The information system also provided a means to locate quickly the expertise within the EPA organization on a broad range of topics. Officials could identify specific expertise from among the hundreds of Ph.D.'s working for the agency, or for contractors and academic institution grantees funded by the agency. The EIS allowed EPA headquarters to locate and tap the experts on subjects ranging from oil-drilling mud to radio waves. This capability was especially valuable to an organization oriented more toward short-term fire-fighting than toward long-range planning.

The EPA information system also allowed headquarters executives to review laboratory-level research projects prior to visits to the facilities. Executives were provided with listings, sorted by organization and individual researcher, of the latest status of every research project being conducted at the laboratory. The executive could then discuss a researcher's work in some detail.

In addition, having the project-level information available allowed management to compare research plans to actual activities. This scrutiny encouraged laboratory researchers and managers to be more responsive to priorities set by headquarters.

Improve Communications

"Build me a system that gets me up-to-date information on our competitors' prices and activities, and you can write your own ticket," summed up a vice-president of marketing's assignment to his new EIS director. His statement illustrates the fact that the higher one rises in an organization, the more important external information sources become. During the late 1970's, the White House interviewed top executives of several dozen corporate giants, asking where these executives procured the key information on which they relied to direct the organization. The answer: more than 90 percent of the important information came from newspapers, telephone calls, and informal discussions with peers.

An effective EIS will not only improve communications within an organization, but also between that organization and the outside world. Outside information, gathered from various sources, on what competitors and major clients are doing, have done, and are planning to do, becomes available in an outward-looking EIS. The EIS that delivers competitive information is the closest most executives will get to eavesdropping on the competition's strategy meetings.

Examples abound. The EIS at an aerospace firm tells the company executives the current levels of competitors' workloads and order backlogs. That lets the firm make very smart pricing decisions on its proposals. In the soft-drink industry, Coca-Cola and Pepsico battle each other using executive-level graphic summaries highlighting where the competition is weak or weakening. In California, a bank monitors its competitors' deposits, by branch, looking for trends and opportunities to exploit.

An EIS also can improve internal communications. Many corporations have found that the electronic mail capabilities of their EIS systems are more than enough to justify the entire system. Executives are inherently busy people. Most of their time is spent in meetings or on telephone calls. This means that they are often unavailable to others in the organization.

Electronic mail systems allow executives to respond to inquiries or other information at their convenience. Some executives use their electronic mail systems to do two things at once. They engage in a telephone conversation with one party while, at the same time, initiating or responding to an electronic mail message on their desk terminal.

A solid example of the economic impact of these systems occurred when the president of a New Jersey pharmaceutical company learned of a pricing and promotion initiative being offered by its principal competitor. Immediately, the executive broadcast an electronic mail message to *every* one of his sales offices telling them just how to counter the competitor's move. Within fifteen minutes, some salespeople were on the phone making the counter-offers. In many cases, they contacted the clients with a better offer before the competitor's salespeople had even called.

Another problem relieved by an EIS is illustrated by the oft-heard lament, "Why do we have to wait three hours to answer a simple question when all the information is stored in computers?" As time passes, the value of information degrades rapidly, especially at the executive level. The importance of rapid access to up-to-date information can be illustrated by the experience of the U.S. Army Corps of Engineers.

In 1986, when General Delbridge was second in command at the U.S. Army Corps of Engineers headquarters in Washington, D.C., he had an EIS called EASE (Executive Access System Environment) designed for himself and several other executives at the Corps. Our interviews with users identified which components of the system were most important, and why. Most users emphasized the up-to-date project monitoring capabilities of the system. This was unexpected since the Corps EIS only updated its project status information monthly.

Pressed for an explanation, General Delbridge explained: "When a Congressman calls about a project in his district, we can now give him an immediate answer. We used to have to say 'We'll get back to you.' It normally does not matter that the information itself is a few weeks old. What's important is that we can respond quickly."

Making members of Congress feel that an agency is responsive to their needs is of utmost importance to every federal agency. In the final analysis, Congress holds the purse strings, and members sometimes judge an agency as much by how it answers inquiries as by how successful it is at its legislated mission.

Reduce Uncertainty

EIS helps executives to feel more confident about their decisions by reducing the perceived size of the unknown component of any decision. In other words, an effective EIS allows executives to know that they know what they ought to know.

In the executive suite, perception is important. If an executive perceives that there is access to the information needed to support a decision, that decision can be made with greater confidence. Also, if an executive is perceived by subordinates as being knowledgeable, then directions will be followed with greater confidence. Finally, if far-flung segments of the organization perceive the executive to be both interested in and on-top-of their local concerns, then the priorities expressed by the executive will be given greater credence.

The issue here is not the quality of the decisions themselves, but what an EIS can contribute to the confidence with which the executive approaches a decision. One of the greatest enemies of the decision-maker is the second-guesser. This is the individual who believes that, "If only the executive knew what I know, things would be done my way." An EIS can disarm a second-guesser by making it clear that the executive does, indeed, have access to the information that is key to the decision at hand. Here we assume, of course, that the EIS is shared among the appropriate corporate managers.

Assist in Team-Building

One of the primary functions of any executive is to get subordinates to pull together—and in the same direction. Military experts tell us that most often this team-building is a function of two things: the personality of the executive and the clarity of vision of where things should be going. An EIS can't do much to improve a rotten personality, but it can help the executive to define, highlight, and reinforce a specific vision of organizational priorities. This happens in several ways:

—By defining the data and functions to be included in an EIS, the executive clearly indicates priorities.

—By making the EIS data available to others in management, the performance of key sectors of the firm is readily visible to all. The resultant peer pressure encourages folks to "toe the line."

—By highlighting successes and the people responsible for those successes, the EIS can improve commitment.

—By providing everyone with the quality-controlled data at the same time, everyone is dealing from the same deck. What's in the EIS are not *some* facts, they are *the* facts upon which major actions will be based.

—By highlighting specific priority issues and requiring that data be reported on those issues, the EIS can help to institutionalize those priorities within the organization.

—By improving communication through applications such as electronic mail, the EIS can speed the development of consensus within the management team.

—By providing access to outside information sources—such as the competitors' performance data reported to the Securities Exchange Commission, news clips, international exchange rates—executives can help to broaden the perspectives of their top management team and tailor their viewpoint of the competitive environment.

The ability of an EIS to assist an organization to build a sense of teamwork is illustrated by the system developed in 1986 by the U.S. Government Printing Office (GPO). The GPO is the arm of the federal government responsible for getting things printed. Considering the propensity of Washington to generate paper, one can readily imagine the importance of the Government Printing Office.

Each year, the GPO negotiates thousands of printing contracts and is responsible for quality control, printing, and distribution of hundreds of millions of documents. It is, without question, the world's largest printer.

Appointed as Public Printer of the United States in 1986, Ralph Kennickell found a demoralized GPO. In the preceding years, the organization had been torn by labor unrest and shifts in leadership. GPO was held in contempt by the majority of its government clients. In addition, the few accurate economic measures available to judge the performance of the organization painted a gloomy picture.

Three years later much had changed. Employees were more upbeat, unions supported major management initiatives, and clients gave GPO improved marks for quality and customer service. The financial condition was improved as well.

Kennickell gave much credit for the improvements to the executive information system launched early in his tenure. The GPO system monitors the data necessary to tell how well the organization is meeting the goals set by top management. A key factor in the success of this EIS is the fact that EIS terminals were installed not only in executive offices but also on the desks of lower-level supervisors. The terminals displayed quality and responsiveness indicators, on-line, in color graphs throughout the entire organization.

Kennickell explained the decision to broaden access to the EIS with a simple question: "Who do you think gets the work done around here?" GPO's executive information system demonstrates that when lower-level managers know what senior management expects of them, and can see how well they are doing, they do their jobs well.

Justifying an EIS: What Will It Cost?

Can the money spent on an EIS be justified by bottom-line calculations? By what criteria should the cautious executives decide how much to invest in such systems?

To a great extent, how much you will be able to get out of an EIS depends upon how much you invest in it. Today's EIS systems can start at $10,000 for a personal computer, data analysis and graphics programs, an EIS delivery program, and a graphics printer. The more sophisticated a system becomes, the more it costs. Two federal agencies, the Department of Commerce's National Oceanic and Atmospheric Administration (NOAA) and the General Services Administration (GSA) each invested more than $1.5 million for EIS software, hardware, and consulting services. In the private sector, a giant financial services company ticketed more than $3 million for a multi-year EIS quest.

In preparing this book, we reviewed, in detail, more than one hundred EIS implementations, and identified a few major decision points which influence the eventual cost, and success, of an executive information system.

These decision points are your choice of: *tools*, the EIS components chosen and the percentage of those components which the firm already has and need not purchase; *consultants*, the way consultants are chosen and used; *focus*, how long it takes to focus the system on the real business problems; *analytical capabilities*, the quality of the tools and the skill of the people assigned to extract, combine and analyze the information for display through the EIS; and *longevity*, an EIS is not a one-shot investment—continuing support is needed, and modifications are inevitable.

We will deal with EIS hardware and software issues in later chapters. In general, however, the best hardware for an EIS is often the hardware you already have in-house. Organizations that purchase new mini- or mainframe computers for EIS have no greater chance of success, and normally have far greater costs, than those that use hardware they already have.

The choice of EIS software is equally important in determining the overall cost of the system. A strong delivery system is only part of the EIS software picture. The best software choices combine the strongest database, analytical, and graphing components with a good delivery system

Experienced consultants can reduce both costs and time to implement, especially during the prototype development phase. Sometimes consultants can be used to identify your business problem or EIS software, but those decisions are usually better made in-house. Consultants also can ease the process of integrating the entire system, setting up automatic systems to pull data from multiple files, and integrating them into the EIS. EIS development is a relatively new skill, and, in most cases, a broad range of EIS experience can be obtained only through established consulting firms.

Trust Me vs. The Bottom Line

An EIS provides an organization with both intangible and tangible benefits. Sometimes a system is launched based upon intangible needs alone, such as when an executive sees an EIS as necessary for effective control of the organization. Or an executive can feel that an EIS is essential to enhance understanding of the business and, hence, the confidence level of decision-making.

Although intangible justifications are valuable, experience has shown that they are insufficient to maintain an EIS after the original sponsor departs the organization. In the example of the Environmental Protection Agency's research project information system, discussed above, departure of the executive who demanded that the EIS be developed left responsibility for the system in the hands of people with no direct need for, or commitment to, the system. So, they dissolved it.

In contrast, an EIS with continuing hard-dollar justifications will usually become more integrated in, and essential to, the functioning of the organization. Such systems are more resilient to personnel changes, although some excellent systems have been eliminated by new managers.

How does one define tangible justifications for an EIS? One way is to design the EIS to monitor a critical transformation, or improvement, required of the organization. The EIS then becomes an integral part of the process of organizational change. It is looked upon as both harbinger, and component, of a new era for the organization.

For example, one major mid-western bank determined that customer satisfaction was essential to the bank's future performance. Armed with a list of 750 indicators of the greatest concern to its customers, the bank's executives ordered that an EIS be created especially to monitor the progress being made on each of these indicators. EIS displays were updated weekly, and became the centerpiece of management's efforts to improve customer service.

With such a focus on client concerns, quality of service improved and errors declined. Savings from error reduction and improved productivity yielded tangible benefits of more than $4.6 million per year. Bank management credits the EIS for much of this gain. The entire EIS cost less than $500,000 to implement.

Similar bottom-line justification and tangible benefits were produced by the Phillips Petroleum price-tracking EIS and the Government Printing Office's system designed to cut waste and improve service.

Individual Opportunities

Because of an EIS system's potential impact upon an organization, the people who direct EIS development gain a rare level of visibility. This may lead to rapid promotion in their organizations. It is not uncommon for EIS directors to advance over one or two levels of management. Some who were anonymous programmers before building an EIS, suddenly become aides to top executives with the associated power and perks.

Recognition and advancement are not limited to the systems developers. They extend to information system directors. Information systems executives who have built EIS systems have found that the systems open doors and allow them to become peers and strategic business partners with other business executives in their organizations. This is a natural by-product of keeping the EIS relevant to the organization and responsive to the users' needs.

The massive migration of Americans to the West was stimulated by dreams of wealth and by the desire to assert personal independence. In the same way, early EIS development is inspired, in part, by individuals' needs to do something important, to make a difference, and to be recognized and paid for it. That is powerful motivation.

Top Floor, Please

Ever get so involved in thought or a conversation while riding in an elevator that you miss your floor? If you want to use the EIS development process to advance your career, then pay attention to two things: what button to push, and when to get off.

Every career path has its unexpected twists and turns. In general, however, the individuals who turned their EIS development experience to the best career advantage had the following characteristics. They focused on the business problem, not on technology. They were flexible and willing to do whatever it took to get the job done. They were sensitive to personalities and issues of "turf," and avoided making enemies. And they did not seek personal visibility until after their systems had proven their worth. In short, most career advancement comes to those who promote the useful business intelligence the EIS contains rather than the technology it uses.

There are two doors to advancement that developing an EIS can open: advancement within the information systems sector and advancement to top management. Because each situation is unique, we'll present two case studies.

Sandy's ambition was advancement within the information systems profession. She was a junior programmer who wanted to make information systems her career, and, in 1982, she got her first chance to build an executive information system. In the process of building the EIS, Sandy gained dramatic promotions and advanced over two levels of older, more experienced managers. Within six years, she had been promoted to director of applications development and was number two in the entire information systems department.

How did she do it? To a great extent it was by making her name synonymous with information to top management. She became known as the person who could meet the constantly changing expectations of top management even when that meant working at her home terminal until the early morning hours. She was always there when a question arose regarding the EIS.

At the same time, Sandy was careful not to become wed to any single packaged EIS software. She took whatever software was necessary and glued it into the EIS system. By doing this, she avoided excluding individuals or systems and thus avoided making enemies of their champions—the people who helped her received full credit while she absorbed the criticism.

Finally, once the EIS had proven its contribution to her organization, Sandy moved out front. She augmented her busy schedule with talks before outside audiences of information professionals. Within that professional milieu, she gained expertise and became an acknowledged leader in her field. When a position opened up in information systems management, she was the logical choice for the promotion.

Our second case study, Paul, saw executive information systems as a stepping stone to a management position outside of that specialty.

Paul, who had an M.B.A. in marketing and information systems, started out in information systems because the pay was better. When the opportunity presented itself, he volunteered for work in the marketing department. With his background in marketing and awareness of the latest information systems techniques, he seized the opportunity to propose a "competitive analysis system" to the chairman of the firm. Today, Paul is director of a dynamic competitive analysis group.

Paul's approach was simpl—his goal was to move out of information systems and into marketing, so he made certain that his system was seen as marketing-oriented rather than technology-oriented. By calling his project a competitive analysis system rather than an EIS or decision support system, he established his credentials beyond the confines of the information profession.

In the process of building his system, Paul spent many hours with the chairman of the firm whose background was in sales and marketing. The EIS was explicitly designed to reflect the chairman's view of competition. The intent was to develop a system which would hone the talents of the firm's marketing and sales staff by highlighting patterns which otherwise would be invisible, other than to people with the chairman's breadth of experience.

With the emphasis on improving competitive position, the EIS promptly demonstrated its utility by providing high-quality visual displays for executive meetings and for client briefings. Again, Paul's strategy was to emphasize the immediate and practical utility of the EIS to his key client, the chairman.

Whether your goal is to climb within the information systems profession or elevate yourself in other areas of management, developing an EIS is a fine opportunity to let your light shine through.

2 In the Beginning: A Short History of the Art

You are invited to tour the offices of senior executives at Boeing Corporation's Seattle headquarters. Nice offices. On the executive's desk is a computer terminal. The executive demonstrates using the terminal to obtain instant answers to time-sensitive questions and to communicate with peers throughout the corporation. A few keystrokes call up dramatic graphic summaries of the company's major activities and provide instant status information on a vast array of specific projects and products.

The latest in executive information systems, right? Not quite. The year of your visit is 1969! More than twenty years ago, top Boeing executives had terminals which could perform the most important functions of contemporary executive information systems.

Decades ago, when the first computer salesmen from Remington Rand, Control Data Corporation, and International Business Machines (IBM) promoted business computers, they promised two key benefits: more efficient operations and better information for management. Every time they tried to sell a larger machine, the same justifications were used. Hindsight shows they delivered improved efficiency. They were far less successful with the goal of improved management information.

The first applications of computers in business were called transaction systems. They recorded accounting transactions, order-entry transactions, inventory change transactions, payroll transactions, and dozens more. Over the years, transaction systems evolved to do more than simply improve efficiency. They became the infrastructure of the firms they served. In modern corporations, turning off the computer that runs the transaction systems would be the equivalent of turning off the lights and sending home the employees. Firms would cease to operate.

A few innovative information systems executives took transaction systems a step further and created a new category of computer applications called strategic systems. One well-known example is American Airlines AAdvantage. Simply an expanded transaction system, AAdvantage was developed to award frequent flyers by recording mileage and sending status reports. Another strategic transaction-based system is Frito-Lay's driver support system. Each day, every day, ten thousand Frito Lay drivers visit the stores where Frito-Lay products are sold. Each driver has a hand-held data recorder which is used to record the quantity of each product that is still on the shelves.

Returning to the truck, the driver plugs the data recorder into a computer. In a few seconds, out comes a complete re-stocking list, to tell the driver what to put on the shelves, and a bill for the store owner. The computer monitors each store's sales by day, so each store is stocked only with the items which are most likely to sell that day. Thus, the stores are better served, the customers get what they want, fresh each day, and Frito-Lay sells more chips.

Management information systems directors and their superiors are being pressured to look for strategic applications from vendors and consultants. IBM and Digital Equipment, for example, are both trying to get their clients to implement systems like those at American Airlines and Frito-Lay because that will increase the value of, and demand for, their computers. At the same time, MIS consultants are pushing their clients toward strategic systems.

This trend is best summarized by Professor Warren McFarland of Harvard Business School. "Corporations should switch their information systems strategy," McFarland is quoted in a *Computerworld* interview, "from one of stamping on mice, or performing clerical tasks, to one of hunting for elephants, or getting the edge on industry competitors."

Strategic systems, and their predecessors the transaction systems, provide real value. While not full-fledged executive information systems, they provide the raw material—the data—on which many an EIS will depend.

The Power of Information

When we say "information is power," we normally refer to the *substance* of the information rather than its format. With the advent of early management information systems, a subtle change began to take place. The *form* of the information, and the mere fact of its rapid availability on an automated system, began to influence the way executives managed. In other words, the form of the information gained considerable power.

What made the Boeing system, mentioned earlier, so much more effective at delivering management information than other early EIS efforts? First, the Boeing system was on-line, and it created and delivered only the reports the executives requested. Users were spared the burden of leafing through reams of unwanted reports to find the data they needed.

Second, the Boeing system presented the data graphically, making trends immediately apparent. The system displayed trends against a backdrop of the goals and budgets for the subject being reviewed. A quick glance told the executive how well the project was doing.

Third, the Boeing data was timely. It avoided the delays associated with accounting data by relying instead on daily time cards and material requests. Time-card data was converted into dollars based upon formulae which, while not perfect, were certainly good enough to identify trends. Information that was almost correct and available overnight was far more valuable than perfect data that you had to wait a month to get.

NASA's Moon Mission, the First EIS?

There have been any number of systems nominated for the title of *The First On-line EIS*. We have decided to award this honor to the system developed by Boeing to support the National Aeronautical and Space Administration (NASA) 1960's effort to get Americans from Florida to the moon. We chose the moon mission for three reasons. First, it is a civilian effort and we can talk about it. Other early EIS efforts were highly classified security projects. Second, it was a valuable EIS, essential to its mission, and it worked. Third, it's our book.

Since the Manhattan Project, which designed the first atomic bomb, military projects have dominated advanced computing technologies. As weapons systems became more and more sophisticated, so did the computers needed to design and run them. It was natural, therefore, that military contractors be among the first to find management uses for computing power.

NASA's moon mission provided the perfect garden for growing an EIS. The project had a clearly defined goal. Management needed to know its status on almost a daily basis. The people doing the work knew computers, and many of the contractors had experience building information systems for the military. By

1969, some of the people responsible for the moon mission had information support systems that merited the title *executive information systems.*

To go to the moon, you have to start somewhere. President John F. Kennedy pledged in the early 1960's to go to the moon "not because it is easy, but because it is difficult." At the time of Kennedy's pledge, the U.S. space effort was playing catch up to the Russians. When it came to space firsts—first earth satellite, first man in space, first man to orbit the earth—Russia owned the record book.

So how did this brash American team hope to go where no man had gone before? It would not be easy. To place one step on the moon required that they complete a hundred thousand steps on the earth—on time. The state of the art in project tracking was paper PERT and Gantt charts produced by complex computer programs that identified critical paths and calculated appropriate schedules. It didn't take long before moon mission management knew that they couldn't get to the moon on a paper airplane. They turned to on-line computer systems.

Boeing initiated the on-line management system as a means of ensuring that it could track its own projects. The costs of building the system were charged to NASA. Upon seeing the system demonstrated, NASA program managers immediately requested access. Boeing was aghast and, instinctively, denied the request. A heated discussion ensued. NASA got to the point of implying that funding would be cut off if access were denied. In the end, both Boeing and NASA executives were given equal, on-line access to the information system.

The revolutionary nature of Boeing's system should not be underestimated. It employed some of the first "intelligent" graphics terminals. Through the 1960's, on-line computer graphics was a central processing unit and core hog. Graphics demanded so much computer power that huge systems were tied up. Just to remain visible, on-screen displays had to be refreshed (redrawn) by the computer twenty or more times each second.

In 1968, breakthroughs from Tektronix, Adage, and others led to smart graphics terminals that could keep pictures visible without demanding the full attention of huge computer resources. Today, of course, every personal computer has a graphics card that provides the smarts for display, but twenty years ago this was hot stuff. Boeing acquired some of these advanced graphics terminals for computer-aided design projects. One of these terminals was drafted for Boeing's executive information system.

The Boeing Tour, 1969

To give you a feel for the environment within which the Boeing developers worked, we'll give you a private guided tour of one of NASA's executive information systems as of February, 1969, seven months before the first humans visited the moon. The tour starts in Seattle, at the Boeing headquarters' computer-aided design center. In those days, sophisticated, computer-aided design graphics were not very impressive by today's standards. To misquote Henry Ford, you could have any color of display as long as it was black-and-white, in two dimensions, and you had endless time to wait for processing between modifications. Boeing had discovered how to make monotone computer equipment into a powerful source of executive-level information.

At the first stop in your tour of Boeing's computer-aided design system, you're shown a landmark computer-generated movie created by Bill Fetter. The movie shows a pilot's view of a simulated aircraft landing on the pitching, rolling deck of an aircraft carrier. While unimpressive compared with 1980's video games, the show is spellbinding in the 1960's.

So realistic is the simulation that the viewer could conjure up a touch of airsickness. Your host drags you away from the movie and up two flights of stairs to the space engineering wing of the building. The next stop is a room in which the surface of the moon has been recreated, at full-scale, just like a movie set. Here movies are made of men moving in space suits to identify flaws in the equipment. Next door is a viewing room where you watch a simulation of the Apollo lunar landing module.

Back to Earth

Then you are introduced to a plain-looking work area with a graphics terminal like the one used in Boeing's computer-aided design facility. "This is our graphical control system," announces your host. "One of our most important systems. On this terminal, we can call up the current cost status and schedule of every one of our NASA projects. It is up-to-date as of last midnight."

At this point, quite frankly, you've still got visions of moon walks and aircraft carriers dancing in your head. You're not really listening. You figure this must be the boring stuff that is required viewing after the fireworks.

Your host presses a few buttons. A three-line graph appears on the screen. The legend indicates that one line is actual spending, one is budget, and one is revised forecast. The horizontal axis shows daily dates at one scale, but can be switched instantly to a weekly or monthly scale. The graph covers from project initiation to project completion. The title box on the graph includes today's date, the name of a component of a missile system, the name of a manager, and a department number.

You begin to wonder how a top Boeing manger could get so excited about a simple chart, when surrounded by simulated aircraft landings and simulated moon orbiting, not to mention one of the most sophisticated computer-aided design systems in the world.

Trying to be polite, you ask who uses the system.

"There is a terminal like this one in the financial manager's office, the office of the vice president in charge of all of our NASA work, and the project manager's office," he's on a roll. "They monitor each of the NASA projects. They can spot problems long before they could if they used end-of-month reports. The graphs show trends, too. Old listings just showed a snapshot."

Like Saul after his trek to Damascus, you finally see the light. This is a revolution!

Now that he has your attention, he continues, "The fellows at NASA in Washington also have terminals hooked into our computer. They start work three hours before we do. By the time our executives get to work, they've already got a stack of telephone messages from the Washington hotshots asking why this is falling behind schedule or that is over budget," he chuckles.

To put the Boeing system in context, recall that, in 1969, up-to-date management graphics was a novel idea. Perhaps a throwback to the gung-ho days of World War II, some firms displayed banners (usually bed sheets) that tracked a single important organization goal. That goal might be production, safety, a blood drive, or the Christmas Club. They updated the banners weekly using a ladder and a red crayon. That was most people's idea of up-to-date management graphics.

As we said, in 1969 the Boeing system was revolutionary.

EIS as Launching Pad

In this context, how important was the NASA moon mission EIS? In the winter of 1980, we talked with James Webb. Webb ran NASA's entire program during the moon mission years. A story-teller at heart, Webb told stories which were rich in meaning. Like Aesop's Fables, each story taught an important lesson.

Recalling the Boeing tour, we asked Webb if all the glitter and pizzazz of the on-line executive information system was really of use. His response was uncharacteristically direct, almost brusque.

"We could not have made it to the moon without the information systems used by Boeing and by our other contractors. Those systems gave our people the kind of up-to-the-minute information we needed to keep the project moving forward." He was convincing. After all, who would know better than the man that analysts credit with putting the first man on the moon?

We'd be delighted to defend the assertion that the systems built to help NASA manage its moon effort were the true first executive information systems. In some ways, they were advanced even by today's standards. For instance, very few of today's EIS systems provide status reports as up-to-date as NASA's daily reports. In other ways, especially presentation graphics, today's systems are far more advanced. But the differences are in the implementation, not in the goals or substance of the systems.

NASA in the 1960's provided the money, the vision, the wisdom, and the rationale to launch the age of executive information systems.

Undercover EIS

Another pioneering EIS effort has not been given the publicity it deserves. That's because it was built for, and used by, a national intelligence agency. In 1976, the agency was developing and experimenting with imaginative ways to present information that executives wanted to see. Much of the information that the agency tracked most urgently was geographic in nature. To make crucial and timely decisions, executives sometimes needed up-to-the-minute information, in excruciating detail, about a particular city or country. They not only needed to know what their agents were doing, but also the context in which it was being done and the major trends influencing the area. In 1976, the agency's computer mapping department was producing executive reports which would be the envy of any modern EIS director.

One of the ways to obtain information from the system was through a graphics terminal. The terminal could display maps of entire countries. Pressing a few keys told the system to zoom in on any section of the country until roads and cities became visible. A few more buttons, and the system showed added detail about specific sites. With the press of another button buildings and waterways appeared. Another display showed civilian resources available for support. All this material was presented on the basic map format, as though the system were placing clear plastic overlays over the map. The effect was inspiring. A few minutes at the map, and you felt that you had a real insight into what was going on in some remote corner of the world.

If you wanted to find out what people and buildings were within a given distance of a particular site, all the operator had to do was draw a circle around the site, and the system would list all the resources located within that circle. Of course, a touch of a button could also highlight the location of competing military resources.

Sounds comprehensive, right? Nonetheless, this was only part of their EIS! The system that served the executives was even more sophisticated. It needed to include not only the maps but also interpretation from the analyst as well. In fact, the EIS was so expansive that it required a whole phalanx of strange-looking computers just to print the reports, and a whole phalanx of analysts to interpret the data. This bank of computers contained, among other things, vast libraries of digitized type fonts or character sets. This extensive library was required to drive a giant optical plotter located in the next room. The computers took the maps and diagrams designed on the graphics terminals and merged them with high-quality lettering to create plates for use in printing.

The room containing the huge optical plotter had to be one of the best secured spots on the face of the earth. Thick walls, no windows and, most importantly, no unwanted external light sources. In the center of the room was a table large enough to serve twelve people in style. Hanging over the table was a small television screen about two inches square. The television screen, or more accurately the cathode ray tube, was suspended from a trolley attached to the ceiling.

The trolley moved silently back and forth over the table, two inches at a time, in near total darkness. Then the tube stopped and projected a picture onto the table where a photosensitive sheet had been carefully spread. It required several hours of exposing to create a plate for printing a complete sixteen page form of the executive information system report.

The agency employees in the room were proud of their technology, but they wouldn't say word one about how it was used. All they would say was that the system created printing plates for an executive report book. The book was never intended for the mass market. Far from it.

Every night, six copies of each new book were printed. Each copy was individually guarded until it reached its target executive. With only six copies in circulation, it is not difficult to imagine who was part of the exclusive executive audience.

What Is Information Worth?

The visit to the intelligence agency can teach the prospective EIS developer a number of important lessons. The most important lesson is that the quality of the presentation should be commensurate with the importance of the information being conveyed. When information is really important, don't skimp on high-quality analysis, graphics, or printing. Be aware of the value of the information.

The agency's information may have started or prevented a war. What would the cost be if one of the six target executives could not understand the information because it was poorly printed on an obsolete piece of computer graphics junk? Surely the problems those six people were facing were important. The survival of people or entire nations may have hung in the balance. Substitute the term "corporation" for the term "nation" in the above sentence, and you are in the proper frame of mind to consider EIS report format. Survival of people becomes survival of jobs. The problems that justify an EIS are also those which are central to the survival of a corporation and to the achievement of the mission of key government agencies.

Where information is important, both quality of analysis, and quality of presentation should reflect that importance.

Another lesson that might be learned from the intelligence agency experience is more subtle. It is still a popular myth that most executives need and demand "what if" tools of their EIS. Such tools allow executives to manipulate alternative scenarios on the screen to find out what would happen if a particular approach were selected. The intelligence agency could, without question, easily deliver the world's most powerful "what if" system. The analysts wanted that type of tool. The executives did not. When it comes to information upon which survival decisions are based, what the nation's busiest executives wanted was the correct information, thoroughly analyzed and validated, clearly presented, and graphically portrayed.

There are undoubtedly some executives who will want to pose alternatives and see the results or want alternative courses of action pointed out to them. However, the executives we have worked with are more interested in what is, not what if. If you work for such a person, you'll have to deliver those tools, also. They simply do not have enough faith in computer models to bet their survival on them. As long as they have the real data, it seems, top executives can use their imaginations to process the "what if" scenarios much more efficiently in the computer between their ears.

Early Efforts and Their Limits

The earliest systems built to inform management (whence the term management information systems) were by-products of the transaction systems. Their reports summarizing financial performance, inventory status, or order trends were produced at the same time that the more detailed listings were printed. The summary reports went to management. The detailed reports went to accountants, inventory control staff, and production supervisors.

When executives received the summary reports, they often saw numbers that raised questions. To answer those questions, the only resources readily available were the original detailed listings. As a result, the executives were left hanging between summary reports, which weren't specific enough, and the detailed reports, which were much too specific. Their questions went unanswered—lost under an avalanche of computer printout.

Throughout the sixties and seventies, data processing department managers tried to respond to the requests of executives. Their first heroic attempts were Cobol-language programs that allowed some flexibility in producing reports summarizing data from financial, inventory, personnel, production, and marketing databases. These databases were created and maintained by the firm's key transaction systems.

Computers could produce more numbers than any human could digest. Perhaps as an outgrowth, a few organizations confused attention to numbers with attention to details such as product quality, consumer trends, and technical advances which were not part of the transaction database. In these cases, management shifted from people who had been around for years and knew *the business* to managers who knew *business*. In the fog of data everything—product, market, personnel—became unclear.

In the executive game, numbers are trump cards. The better the numbers, the greater the advantage. This is fine as long as the numbers available to a firm's executives reflect the full range of indicators of the firm's success. Problems arise when only part of the numbers an organization needs are available. Most transaction numbers indicate short-term status. Because these were the only numbers available, executives had to use them. The result? A short-term focus on factors which did not necessarily represent long-term measures of the organization's success. The main problem with these systems is not that they failed, but that they gave the *appearance* of success. As a result, some organizations were distracted from asking for better, or the right, information.

Most early attempts at producing executive-level information fell short because they were not sufficiently flexible. Each new executive request sent harried Cobol programmers scrambling to force-fit a product. From the executive's viewpoint, the early systems almost invariably suffered from three major problems: (1) they produced too much detail; (2) they hid, rather than illuminated, trends; and (3) they delivered information too late for the executive to use effectively.

Too Much Detail

Developers of early management information systems faced a dilemma that still causes problems today. Their executives were inconsistent in the amount of detail they demanded. One day, the executive would demand all of the detail down to the lowest level of the organization. The next, the executive would have a fit because the management reports were so bulky and it was so difficult to find the key top-level information.

These developers also were programming in complex languages were more appropriate for writing payroll systems or conducting physics experiments than for generating management reports. The batch-processing computers made them wait hours for each test of a new program. The smallest error or modification required another long wait.

What would you do in that situation? Of course, you'd build systems that printed everything, and that's exactly what they did. They figured that it was safer to produce too much rather than to risk not producing enough.

Hiding Trends

Most of the early MIS reports were either listings of budget variances or detailed records of transactions. The budget variance listing showed who was over or under budget and by how much. There were two sets of numbers, one for the month that had just ended and one showing the cumulative total since the beginning of the year. These two numbers were sometimes in different sections of the printout.

Detailed transaction listings were just that. They showed every bill, every order, every delivery, every credit, and every return. The charge for a new office water cooler took equal precedence with the cost of a new oil tanker. Trying to find something significant in those listings was like looking for the proverbial needle in a haystack.

To search through this miasma of numbers and blizzard of printout, top managers recruited talented staffs with M.B.A.'s who studied each report looking for important patterns or trends. Smaller organizations couldn't afford such analytical talent, so their computer listings became convenient doorstops. They knew that somewhere in all that swill lurked pearls of wisdom, but they didn't have the time, resources, or patience to search for them.

Even in the larger organizations, the analysts were crippled by the very format of the data. Trends were obscured by the fact that the relevant data was scattered throughout the printout, or the data was at the wrong level of aggregation, or the time scale was wrong. With automated systems rapidly replacing some of the old timers who knew instinctively what was going on, the fact that the new systems hid trends and allowed problems to fester.

To appreciate this quandary better, look at the following example of a budget variance listing of sales versus quota.

Group	Current Period			Year to Date		
	Sales	Quota	Variance	Sales	Quota	Variance
East	200	200	0	850	850	0
South	200	200	0	850	850	0
West	200	200	0	850	850	0

The table shows that all three sales staffs are identical, performing right on budget, and have been all year long–right? Now look at the three graphs of data below based upon more complete figures fully consistent with the summaries above:

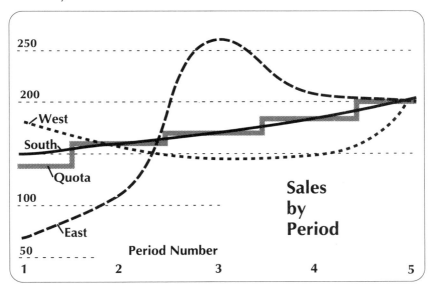

As can be seen from this graph, East was improving dramatically until the fourth period, when things fell apart. West fumbled along until the fifth period, but now seems to be on an upsurge. South appears well managed—its sales track the quota.

Based on the budget variance *listing*, sales were cruising along just fine in all areas. However, based on the *graph* of actual performance, the South is the only group that has remained near quota all year. West was in a slide but has turned around, perhaps because of a new manager. The guy moved from the East where things seem to have taken a nose dive since he left in the third period.

Of course, the actual sales figures for the past five periods, which would no doubt have been hidden several inches down in the listings, were: East; 60, 110, 260, 220, 200. South; 140, 160, 170, 180, 200. West; 180, 170, 150, 150, 200.

Data Arrives Too Late

Many early MIS reports relied upon accounting data as their raw material. Accounting data becomes available, at the earliest, several days after the end of a month. Revenue numbers generally reflect billings rather than sales. Cost data reflect bills received rather than purchases issued. In other words, the data in those MIS reports may reflect business decisions and actions that occurred days, weeks, or months ago. The reports offer no way to find out when the action was taken.

It's like driving a car looking through the rear-view mirror. How can executives act decisively when the data they rely on is outmoded? Frustrated by their inability to get useful information, some executives demanded more and more numbers. The process fed on itself until some organizations were investing valuable organizational talent, skills, and experience generating seemingly endless piles of listings.

Not Under Executive Control

Fourth generation languages and decision support systems emerged in the seventies to make management information systems more responsive. Their goal was to provide access to the right information in the right format. Many succeeded admirably, making it possible to get information graphically, to get it quicker, and to get only the information needed by top management.

Yet these systems did not completely fill the need. In most cases, fourth generation languages and decision support systems were the exclusive domain of the experts who knew how to program them. If the executive wanted to ask a question, he was forced to ask the expert. Learning to use these systems required extensive training—an unwanted drain on scarce executive time.

Fourth generation languages and decision support systems helped get the right information to executives, but they did not allow the executives the power to directly manipulate the systems themselves.

The EIS field emerged partially as a rebellion against overweight, obscure, and outmoded reports, and partially as a means of allowing executives to get the data they needed directly from information systems without requiring either third party assistance or extensive training.

Why EIS Now?

If we have had systems which qualify as executive information systems for more than twenty years, why is it that only now a broad range of chief executives is demanding their own systems? In general, the new interest in executive information systems is the fortuitous confluence of three forces—the availability of information, the availability of computer technology, and the evolution of information-sophisticated executives. The information is now in computers, the delivery systems are in place, and executives understand that EIS is possible.

Information is in computers. For thirty years companies have been spending millions of dollars to automate administrative processes—accounting, manufacturing, sales, customer service, personnel, distribution, and so on. Millions of terminals encode data daily, capturing untold numbers of business transactions.

Systems create data at every step of the business process. For example, a builder may call the sales office of a local distributor to order fiberglass insulation. The distributor's sales clerk turns to a terminal, which is tied directly to the insulation manufacturer's computers. The computer displays availability and price. The clerk conveys this information to the customer, gets approval, and enters the order.

That night, a program at the manufacturer checks the day's orders, updates the sales totals to calculate commissions, projects demand for the coming month, and tells manufacturing how much of each product to produce. A second program transfers the day's orders to an accounting file to update daily financial statements.

These systems are essential. If they suddenly failed, the company's business would grind to a halt. Nothing could be ordered because manual sales entry systems no longer exist. Accounting clerks can operate the computers but would go bonkers if asked to calculate financial statements manually. The volume of detail would soon overwhelm all efforts to manage it.

These systems create data—not just the reports and bills and checks that are their prime products, but millions of data items that are just there, waiting as back-up just in case the primary data files need to be revived. All the systems provide information which, when summarized, can provide grist for the executive information system mill.

Delivery systems are in place. During the personal computer revolution, twenty million small computers appeared on desk tops throughout the world. Executives use many of them, primarily for access to electronic mail. To be more precise, as of 1989, more than twenty percent of senior executives had computers or computer terminals on their desks, and eighty percent of the use was for electronic mail. Those same machines can be used for more ambitious forms of executive information delivery. Moreover, the cost of a personal computer has now dropped below $5,000, a level of expenditure most executives can authorize.

For those executives who refuse to have a computer cluttering their desks, another delivery mechanism has quietly arrived: the high-quality laser printer. The laser printer can produce a book of charts and graphics nearly as easily as it can produce endless numerical listings. Laser-printed chartbooks can be of superb quality. In addition, they are portable, easily distributed, and can be used for daily, or weekly, executive information delivery .

Executives know about EIS. As the NASA moon mission case illustrated, advanced executive information systems have been possible for more than twenty years. Given the dramatic benefits that the EIS could have provided, why didn't more executives demand their own EIS regardless of the cost of information and delivery systems? For one simple reason: They did not know about EIS. Very few people did.

For its first twenty years of existence, business computers were for automating clerical, accounting, and manufacturing functions, not for executives. Unfortunately, that bias was strongly reinforced when the first personal computers showed up in executive offices loaded with Wordstar, VisiCalc, and Lotus 1-2-3. Mastering even the most rudimentary of the early spreadsheet programs required a level of patience and investment of time which were rare in executive offices. Executives believed, quite justifiably, that the investment of time and effort necessary to make a computer useful to them was far larger than they could afford to make. Early personal computers, with arcane spreadsheet and word processing programs, proved to them that they were right.

Computers were for people with the time and desire to become computer experts, not for executives. Executives, in general, have long-term goals but short-term focus.

Times changed. A few innovators built executive information systems. Then their executive clients showed their systems to executives from other companies, who in turn asked for similar systems. Executives were getting more familiar with computers, and computers were getting much friendlier to non-programmers.

In 1984, an EIS software industry emerged. Two pioneers, David Friend of Pilot Executive Software and Richard Crandall of Comshare, bet their companies' futures on the idea that large organizations would invest heavily in systems to keep their top executives informed. After a slow start, the EIS software industry matured and prospered. With prosperity came visibility through advertisements in major business media such as *Business Week.*

It was not until 1988, however, that the editorial side of the business press took serious interest in executive information systems. Frankly, until then, there were two EIS failures for every success, and many of the most successful executive information systems were so important to their owners that information on them was considered corporate confidential.

Then, on a sultry Monday morning in June of 1988, both *Business Week* and the *Wall Street Journal* ran feature articles trumpeting the benefits of executive information systems. Shortly thereafter the *New York Times* did a piece on EIS, and six months later a similar article appeared in *Fortune.* The cat was out of the bag. Executives suddenly knew what they were missing.

EIS is still not a foregone conclusion. Far from it. Each organization, it seems, must undergo its own struggle with the new potentials. Everything from personality to organization identity to internal politics must be grappled with in order to join the ranks of the EIS-blessed. Turf wars among information-oriented staffs (MIS, information center, executive staffs) add an inevitable dose of confusion and frustration. Added to these problems are the attempts of some information systems executives to exploit

EIS as a lever to gain approval for major upgrades to their computer centers. Slapped with a potential $3 million price tag for a new central processing unit, many a top executive has lost the desire for an EIS. The smoke from the turf battles must clear and the information systems executive's Christmas list must be whittled down, before EIS will become a popularly used information technology.

Once it is unleashed, EIS is like a weapon. Aimed at the right target, it can have tremendous impact. If poorly aimed or otherwise misused, however, that same weapon can be useless if not downright hazardous. This book is written to help you to aim your EIS.

EIS Pioneers

The great executive information system pioneers display a rare combination of vision and practicality. They are stargazers with feet firmly planted. The EIS pioneers needed to be visionaries in order to see beyond the arguments put forward by technologists about why what they wanted could not be done. They ignored the nay-sayers and just set out in their own direction. But they remained practical enough to avoid becoming enamored with new technology. They fixed their eyes on the ultimate goal of the EIS—to make more profit for the stockholders or to provide more effective services for the taxpayers.

We haven't determined who envisioned Boeing's system. Whoever they are, they would be at the head of our class. One of the pioneers we do know is Courtney Jones. Jones is chief financial officer at Merrill Lynch.

When he was treasurer of General Motors Corporation, Jones faced a problem. GM was transferring, to Detroit, the New York-based subsidiary that had been making the chartbooks for GM's board of directors and the visuals for GM board meetings. Most of the people and functions had to be replaced.

Jones felt that computers could be used to automate much of the graphic-designers' work, but he also had a vision of a future in which the executive could touch a few buttons on a computer terminal and get more up-to-date information than could be obtained from the paper-based system produced by the staff of analysts. In 1979, he told his assistant to create a system to produce the necessary visuals and, using the same technology, create an on-line delivery system he could use himself.

Throughout the effort, Jones was involved. He ensured that the needed resources were available. Jones followed through by participating in discussions essential to making the graphic summaries of key indicators a success, and he opened the doors to the necessary information. And the reports and graphics were available at the touch of a button.

In the past decade, the system Jones created has grown and matured, and, in a much modified form, is still in use at GM. Jones has created a similar system at Merrill Lynch.

There were a dozen other pioneering executives who knew technology could be a partner in managing their organizations, and were willing to spend large amounts of money to prove that they were right. We have not the space to mention all of them, but wish to acknowledge their contributions.

EIS Jargon: Drill Down or Belly Up?

Like every other intellectual exercise, the executive information systems field has already generated its own vocabulary. If, at first, this vocabulary appears perplexing to the uninitiated, it is supposed to be so. After all, if the capabilities and methods of EIS were readily understood, what would the EIS experts do?

We won't pretend to offer an extensive tour of the terms applied to executive information systems. In fact, we've not used all these terms in our book, but have included them here so they won't be new when you encounter them. The following are some of the more colorful definitions used in the clash of the EIS jargonauts.

Belly up: This is not a term that you want used in reference to your executive information system.

Boardroom-quality graphics: High-resolution, high-quality graphics that can easily be changed in response to the tastes of the executive clients. The better the graphics, the broader the smile on the boss's face.

Closed EIS: An EIS that can deliver only graphs or reports which were created by the EIS software itself.

Drill down: A means of calling for another level of detail while looking directly at a report or graph.

EIS director: The technically knowledgeable individual who integrates data, software, and hardware into a working EIS, usually by leading a team.

Exception reporting: A tabular or graphic variance report showing some numbers in different colors, or highlighted, or with an asterisk next to them, or simply a line or bar drawn to distinguish that it has exceeded some threshold.

Executive: A person who has an important mission to accomplish and substantial staff and/or other resources with which to carry out their mission.

Executive information system: An information delivery and communication system which supports the needs of top managers. Read this book.

Executive workstation: A terminal or personal computer with the right boards, communications, and peripherals to run the executive information system.

Graphic user interface: Computer software that displays pictographs, reports, and charts and responds to user selections made by pointing with a mouse or a touch screen.

Hot spots: Locations on a display that can be selected by the viewer for additional action. Selection is usually made using a mouse or touch screen.

Hypertext: A method of integrating data and programs which allows the user to easily access greater levels of detail about whatever information is being displayed. Access is via a pointing mechanism. See Mouse.

Intangible benefits: The benefits ascribed to an EIS by "experts" and promoters who do not know how to justify executive information systems. Consider compensating such experts for their advice in "intangible" dollars.

Local area network (LAN): A set of electrical cables, equipment, and software that allows personal computers to communicate with each other, with minicomputers, or with mainframes. Such networks allow users to share comments or files and permit a few programs to serve all the people connected to the network.

Mouse: A rodent-sized, computer input device that slides along the desk and controls a pointer on the computer screen. The user indicates choices by pointing and pressing a button.

On-line EIS: Part or all of the information delivered by the EIS comes to the executive through a personal computer or terminal screen attached to the computer. The alternative is a paper-based EIS.

Open EIS: EIS that can deliver any text, reports, or graphs produced by any software package.

Prefabricated EIS: See Closed EIS.

Stoplight charts: Graphic displays showing status information in three categories—far off-target in red, slightly off-target in yellow, on-target in green.

Touch screen: A sensing device on a computer screen that can sense the pressure of a user's touch and the location on the screen that was touched, and respond appropriately.

Trend analysis: A graph showing a set of hourly, daily, weekly, monthly, or yearly data points with a line fitted to them.

3 Ingredients of Success: Need a Bigger Boat?

In the film classic *Jaws*, when the monster shark first appears, it dwarfs the shark-hunters' boat. Terrified, the film's hero gasps, "Yer gonna need a bigger boat." He was right. He was also a bit late. When pursuing something as challenging as an EIS (or a 26-foot Great White Shark), be sure to plan carefully *before* you set sail. Be prepared.

The goal of this preparation is *not* to pre-program your EIS journey. That cannot be done. EIS *is* the journey, not the goal. Preparation should be aimed at ensuring that your system maintains enough flexibility and responsiveness to meet the real and changing needs of the organization and the EIS sponsor. Don't wait until you're dead in the water, miles from shore, and surrounded by hungry sharks to realize how useful it would have been to have built in a flexible backup system.

An EIS is both evolutionary and revolutionary. It is evolutionary in that it responds to changing demands, goals, and conditions. EIS development is a process of prototype, feedback, and adjustment that continues throughout the life of the system.

An EIS is revolutionary in that it can do certain things for top management better than ever before. Top management has always needed to know what's going on, both inside and outside of the organization. An EIS can help provide this insight without depending upon spies or subjective sources. As such, a good EIS can be the crucible wherein the art and the science of management are united. Hot stuff.

No wonder some folks are intimidated. Implementing an EIS is equal parts experience, skill, timing, and luck. Three of these you control. One you may or may not.

In this chapter, you'll gain a wealth of experience from the real-life examples we provide. There's no substitute for experience to provide the insight necessary to avoid errors and seize opportunities. In these case studies, the experiences speak for themselves. In addition, our dos and don'ts will help you to gain insight into the EIS development process.

The rest is up to you.

The Four Essentials

There are four overwhelming essentials to a successful EIS: having an active, supportive executive sponsor; selecting the right business problem; developing a useful prototype; and maintaining a flexible and responsive system. Highlights of these three essentials follow.

Having an active, supportive executive sponsor allows the EIS developer to obtain the other essentials. The executive helps identify the business problem, gets the resources needed, and makes certain that the right people have access to the EIS.

Selecting the right business problem means choosing an objective whose inherent value is far greater than the cost of the executive information system designed to address it. If not provided by the sponsoring executive, the business problem may be found in the annual operating plan. Look for a business objective based upon a problem which can be solved, at least in part, by improved use and distribution of information. More on this later.

Developing a useful EIS prototype takes into consideration the entire give-and-take process through which the system is made effective for its executive users. It is only through interacting with the users that a responsive and effective system can be achieved.

Maintaining a flexible and responsive system means, quite simply, saying "yes" when the executive sponsor asks for a few changes or new EIS functions. Saying "no can do" only a few times makes both the EIS developer and the system seem less effective than the human-supported system the executive knows and trusts. Software is the key to flexibility, and is theme of a later chapter.

The above four essentials are of such generalized importance that each is covered, at length, later in this book. Here, we highlight some other factors that contribute to a successful EIS, and debunk some prevailing EIS mythology.

Is Size a Factor?

There are a few pursuits in which size is a key factor. Until recently, this was true of executive information systems. An EIS was expensive to build, and was highly specialized in application. Only the most complex and sophisticated operations could justify one, and only the wealthiest could afford one.

All this has changed in the past two years. The costs for EIS building blocks have dropped dramatically, and more people have learned EIS development skills. Now there is a different, if more complex, set of factors which combine to influence EIS development. Factors such as the size of an organization are now secondary. More important are the broader issues: the need for standardized information, for rapid information retrieval and dissemination, and for access to an array of internal and external data sources. Like the computer before it, the EIS is leaping from the privileged few to the enlightened many.

With recently available hardware and software, the size of an organization has become far less important to a successful EIS. In its place is the scope of the executive's vision. Where the organization stands *today* is only part of the picture. Even more important is where the sponsoring executive wants the organization to be in six months, or two years. The EIS can help turn this vision into a reality.

The size of an organization does influence the range of applications for its EIS. For example, large organizations often incorporate competitive data-analysis capabilities and external economic data into their EIS. Small organizations don't. Some large aerospace company EIS's monitor military funding levels, competitors' backlogs and profits, in addition to project management and profitability. Smaller aerospace companies, on the other hand, usually limit EIS focus to project management and profitability.

Another major difference between EIS systems for large versus small organizations is the relative availability of software expertise. Large organizations field teams of internal business systems consultants ready and able to assist managers in creating information systems to meet individual needs. These people can be a big help in getting an EIS off the ground. By way of contrast, smaller organizations have fewer unallocated resources and will normally buy their EIS assistance from outside consultants.

Large multinational and multisite organizations find electronic mail systems central to their EIS efforts. Single-site organizations often skip the electronic mail component. The exception to this latter rule is the organization where executives often are away from the office. In those cases, electronic mail can boost productivity by reducing the time wasted in playing "telephone tag."

How large must a firm be to benefit from an EIS? You may be

surprised. A consulting firm of only sixty employees and $4 million in revenue benefits dramatically from an EIS which helps to allocate key staff members among a number of projects. Their EIS also maintains up-to-date projections of the workload for each staff member.

The EIS helps the firm in two ways. First, the firm avoids promising more than can be delivered. The EIS provides proposal writers with information on who is and is not available. Second, the EIS is a valuable marketing tool. It is seen as an impressive display of the firm's overall capabilities.

Know Your Data

Another difference between executive information systems in large and small organizations is the kind of problems you will encounter in gathering EIS information. Large organizations have more automated systems and, therefore, many more data sources. They also have been developing information systems for a longer time and may have several unique systems. In large organizations, the needed EIS data may be in files maintained by custom-built information systems, whose data structures were crafted by long-departed wizards.

Yesterday's ingenious solutions to data processing problems can become today's EIS nightmare. For example, one well-established firm had been using computers since the early 1960's. The current EIS data expert attempted to extract data from the firm's key financial management system by reading the print files it created. Some time in the dim past, an ingenious programmer had constructed an algorithm to check pages for the longest number in each column, and then set the column widths *for each page* so that they precisely fit the numbers—looked neat—drove the EIS expert buggy.

The EIS expert labored for two weeks to develop a sophisticated procedure to get around the meandering column widths. After completing an elegant fix she discovered, deep within the financial management system printout, that not all of the pages had the same set of columns. For example, rather than enter "no data" in space allocated to a new or discontinued operation, the report deleted the column entirely. Back to the drawing board.

To overcome the multi format data problems of large organizations, your EIS team will need access to highly skilled data readers to build bridges between existing data systems and the EIS.

On the other hand, some smaller organizations using packaged software applications will find that the data in their computer systems is in standard file formats. Most EIS software can read standard formats easily. However, in other small organizations, much of the data needed for EIS will not even be on a computer. To get the data the EIS needs, those organizations will require that clerks enter the data.

Large organizations are more likely to get their EIS data from the host computer. Smaller organizations, with less sophisticated host computer applications, often collect the data from personal computers. Personal computer programs may use some of the data available on the host computer, but usually reformat and rearrange it to meet the needs of the individual user.

The data needed for an EIS will be found only partially in the database the organization maintains. Especially in larger organizations, much of the data will be in files kept by staff who are responsible for providing executives information in various areas. These people already extract data, or gather it from outside sources. They then use an analysis program such as Lotus 1-2-3 or FOCUS to get the executive-level information they need. These people, with their data, often form the core of a new EIS.

The most useful EIS data sources are more likely to be the results of analyses developed by staff rather than new data extracted from large files. In time, the EIS may automate some or all of the analytical functions. But at the beginning, their information can give the EIS a jump start.

Need for Consistent Information

One of the quickest ways to derail an executive-level decision session is to show up with *new* information which contradicts that distributed for the meeting. Such unexpected information, if inconsistent with older information, can pull the rug out from under management's current strategy. In addition, the very appearance of an unexpected dose of data can derail the entire discussion and undermine confidence in any decision.

Large organizations are full of inconsistent data. The four major sources of inconsistent data are: errors in data gathering, deviations in data timeliness, varying definitions of key terms, and multiple programs summarizing the same data differently. Nobody's perfect. Errors in the data gathering and reporting process can and do occur. A minor error in a new program can introduce a difficult-to-detect bias in the data. Even older programs can produce some surprises when faced with new types or sources of input. You will need to identify and weed out error sources before the data in your EIS will be trustworthy. This can cause the data entry phase of EIS projects to take far longer than might appear necessary at first glance.

Deviations in the timeliness of data are a common source of executive-level conflicts. During program review meetings, people responsible for gathering the background information are always at a disadvantage. The data sources are usually the managers of divisions whose efforts are being reviewed. Those managers always seem to arrive at the meeting with more "up-to-date" information which, not coincidentally, makes them look better. An EIS can help to eliminate this problem by defining one source for each key indicator, and by making information available to everyone at the same time.

Different definitions for key indicators can undermine management efforts to communicate. As an example, consider that the federal government has a half-dozen ways to describe different stages of spending money. There are appropriations, authorizations, commitments, obligations, payments, and so on. That's one of the reasons it is so difficult to find out how much the government is spending.

The same proliferation of definitions plagues corporations as well. For instance, should a sale be counted when an order is received? When the order is shipped? When the customer receives the material? When payment arrives?

A 1986 meeting of the board of directors of a public company illustrates: During the meeting, one of the directors complained, "Half an hour ago, Contracts told us to expect $15.3 million in sales during the last quarter. Then Sales came in and said the number was $17.1 million. Then the chief financial officer said it was just under $14 million. Would you guys just pick a number, any number?"

The frustrated director did not want to know that maintenance revenue was not completely bookable and that only sixty percent of new contracts were booked upon shipment. All he wanted was for the corporate officers to work from the same data so that the board could provide the advice they were being paid to provide. One way for an EIS to be useful is to force a consistent definition of key terms on the organization and to make it clear what the terms mean.

The politics behind data often presents major barriers to EIS implementation. Inside an organization, power and influence derive from having the best, most accurate, and most recent figures. After all, how can you be in the know if you don't know anything special? Managers seldom give up their proprietary definitions and data sources without a fight.

The fight usually involves a central group such as finance or management information systems, and a department controller or manager who has created an individual data analysis system. That system may use corporate databases, but process the data differently from how the centralized analysis system reports it.

The department manager will claim that a pet information system is superior because the centralized system is inflexible and cannot provide the data needed to run the department. The keepers of the centralized data acknowledge that the departmental manager's system is better suited to that department's needs, but assert the need for a single, common data repository. The senior executive, who just wants to know what the numbers are, is caught in the middle.

A New England bank struggled with this problem after its president threatened several executives with dire consequences if they could not agree on one set of numbers. The financial manager found the answer by creating an EIS which gave the departmental executives all of the views of the data that they wanted. At the same time, the EIS maintained a common data base and a common reporting system in order that everyone would get the same answer when they asked the same question.

In the process, the EIS completely remodeled existing reporting systems by including every manager's most trusted report formats as options within the centralized system. Any manager could look at any other manager's view of the data. The departmental managers, despite giving up their proprietary data sources, found a silver lining. When the financial office maintained the reporting system, one or more people were freed from that task within each department. In effect, the new system added to each department's available staff.

In creating the revised system, the managers at last came to terms with each other on a common set of definitions. As one of the bank's senior executives summed it up, "Now we spend our time discussing the issues, not fighting over the data."

Nothing is more annoying to most executives than the unexpected. If your EIS is firmly founded on the perception that current information sources are inconsistent, and your system can solve the problem, your chances of success near 100 percent.

Need for Speed

A short time *after* the United States and England signed the Treaty of Paris ending the war of 1812, the two countries actually fought one of the biggest battles of that war. Andrew Jackson's homespun troops humiliated the British forces at the Battle of New Orleans. Had information moved more swiftly in those days, the British would have saved many lives and considerable military dignity.

The speed with which an EIS brings important information to an executive is another key ingredient for EIS success. If your sponsoring executive says, "If only I had known sooner . . ." about a bit of missed information, there's an opening for your EIS.

At Phillips Petroleum, an EIS helped former President Robert Wallaceto earn an extra $50 million for the company by getting him a bit of data before anyone else. Wallace's EIS monitored petroleum prices, following the sun from the Middle East around the world to the Orient. Late one afternoon, he looked at the patterns in his EIS graphs, and spotted an anomaly. Early next morning, he immediately checked the Middle East oil market. The suspicious pattern recurred. He knew it was not a fluke.

In response, he called one of his petroleum traders and told him to buy a particular type of crude oil. The trader indicated no need to buy the crude. Wallace *ordered* him to do so. That single decision earned Phillips $50 million in one day.

An EIS also can provide more rapid access to internal data. Many companies, for example, no longer need to wait for the end of the month to report progress to top managers. At an east-coast engine manufacturer the president's EIS provides daily status information on every order and on every batch of engines the company makes. Daily information allows the president, and the top lieutenants, to catch problems early and to reallocate manufacturing resources more quickly.

In any large international corporation, currency exchange rates can play an important role in determining overall profitability. At one large multinational, the firm's treasurer had the staff monitor Reuters's financial data service. *Every two hours*, the treasurer received an updated report of exchange rate trends. These reports were detailed listings of currency rates for the previous month, week, day and each hour of the current day.

A lot of data, to say the least. In 1981, the firm created an EIS. The new EIS consists of graphic display terminals located on the treasurer's and assistant treasurer's desks. The clear new displays highlight price trends, reduce errors, and require much less time for the executives to interpret. In addition, each of the displays is updated *every fifteen minutes*! The EIS has become a trusted tool of managers who must make decisions about international currency movements on a minute-by-minute basis.

At the other extreme, many EIS systems go unused for lack of speed. At one government agency, for example, the executives who should have been using the EIS weren't. They complained that they could get more timely information from other sources and, therefore, had no reason to consult the EIS.

The Art of Packaging

Speed of information means two things: rapid *access* to the information and effective *packaging* for quick uptake by key executives. Just having access to the information is of little use if that information is so hopelessly buried that it never gains top-level visibility. For example, U.S. forces had all of the information necessary to anticipate and defend against the Japanese attack upon Pearl Harbor in 1941. That information was never conveyed to the top echelons in a form that got their attention until hours after the U.S. Pacific fleet had been pulverized.

Consider another war front: the Cola Wars. Pepsi's battle for supremacy on the supermarket shelves illustrates how the formatting of data is a crucial component of ensuring the utility of that data to top managers. Pepsi, like its competitors, subscribes to market research services that count the number of cases of each brand purchased in each metropolitan area. The data is voluminous. Each month it easily fills box after box of listings. In this format, the data is of little use to senior executives.

In the late 1970's, top executives at Pepsi decided upon an

aggressive strategy. They determined to invest heavily to increase their market share over Coke. They appreciated that the market research data was the only way to know who was winning, and that it was also the most effective information to help them to decide where to invest promotional resources.

Pepsi called in its information systems managers. In short order, they recommended transforming the market research data into graphic formats. The new formats showed how Pepsi was doing against its major competitors in 300 television marketing areas. When the top executives saw the first results from their new EIS, they were enthusiastic. And they became involved. Over the next five months, the executives worked with the EIS staff to design an impressive set of multipart graphic displays. The displays clearly showed changing consumer buying patterns. The same patterns were barely decipherable from the listings. The information systems department appreciated speed as well as packaging. They set up the EISso that the volumes of market research data were automatically converted into

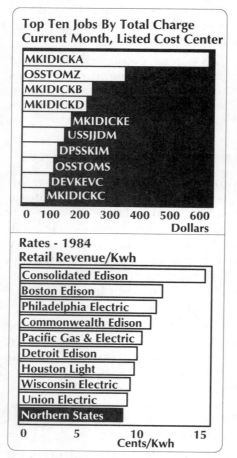

Numerically sorted bar charts are nearly always better than charts sorted by alphabet. Numerical order makes rankings clearer.

In the lower of the two charts to the left, the format for which was supplied by Northern States Power, helps the reader to find the important bar by highlighting it with tint while the other bars are left in standard format. The effect is more dramatic in color.

the graphic formats as soon as the data arrived at the company. The system delivered those graphs, in both paper and 35mm slide formats, to the executives responsible for the market-share improvement program.

According to the EIS project staff, the new format reduced—from five days to one—the time required to respond to opportunities. The key was the system's ability to highlight important evolving patterns. The executives credit this time saving and the insights offered by the graphics with giving them an important competitive advantage. They saw more, saw it earlier, and could act on it more quickly.

Packaging means more than graphics in the form of bar or line charts. It also means highlighting numbers in tables so that they will draw the executive's attention. Packaging also can mean selecting and displaying only those elements of information that are critical. All three packaging techniques—graphing, highlighting, and selecting—are valuable, but only if they are applied to the correct indicators.

What to Display?

The Pepsi experience is an excellent illustration of our next point: The importance of merging effective display with the careful selection of key indicators. The choice of what to display goes hand in hand with the choice of how it is displayed.

Pepsi's graphic-formatting project worked because it used effective graphics (comparative trend charts) and because the people working on the project knew what information to extract. It's a simple problem in logic, with a one-in-four chance of success. The three wrong choices are: *good* displays of the *wrong* indicators, *bad* displays of the *wrong* indicators, and *bad* displays of the *right* indicators. Of course, the key is to make *good displays of the right indicators.*

How do you select the right indicators? The right indicator has five key characteristics. The first four are: it influences the success of the organization, it is measurable, it is updated at brief intervals, and management can act on it. Without all of these characteristics, the indicator probably can't help management todetermine, let alone improve, conditions. Some of the best indicators are those that monitor quality and customer service. They allow simple measures such as the number of items rejected, or the number of customer complaints.

The fifth key characteristic of a good EIS indicator is that the information it presents is compared with some standard. Numbers presented alone rarely serve management's needs. This is true of most figures that come from transaction-based accounting or manufacturing information systems. To be an effective management indicator, data must be related to some important standard of success, or of failure.

Good indicators must be shown in relation to a key management goal, a minimum acceptable standard, or both. In financial reporting, for example, the budget often is considered to be the standard. It is all well and good to make financial data into an EIS indicator, but an effective EIS goes even further. Executives also need to know what the data means in terms of the goal or goals they set. For instance, if minimum acceptable performance is no more than a ten percent variance from budget, the EIS should enable the executive to focus on a fifteen percent variance instantly, without being distracted by a bunch of five percent variances.

One effective differentiation tool is the performance zone. Performance zones are often color-coded. In one sales-oriented company's EIS, for example, if departmental costs are less than one percent over budget, they are in the green performance zone. Between one and ten percent over budget, they are assigned to the yellow zone. More than ten percent over budget, they enter the red zone.

The consistent use of color in an EIS lets executives know instantly which departments are in which performance zones. Such an EIS can save executives the time they would otherwise waste digging through numbers they don't need to see. On the facing page is a black and white stoplight chart. Refer to the illustrations later in this book for an example of a performance-zone stoplight illustration which uses color to convey information.

An EIS can also transform raw numbers into effective indicators by presenting both the specific goals and the minimum acceptable performance on one chart. Performance parameters appear as background information on each chart, with the actual raw data placed on the chart in the appropriate position relative to the performance standards. This type of chart combines the best of both worlds: precise data maped onto instantly recognizable performance standards.

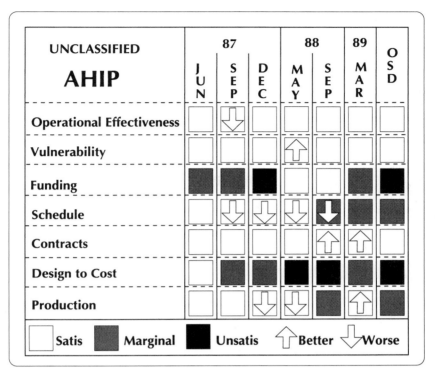

In the classic black-and-white stoplight chart, illustrated above, a simple set of symbols allows each element of the chart to be clearly tagged with indications of both status and trends. One advantage of stoplight charts is that they are very to skim for important information.

When graphic indicators are used to display non-financial data, some executives find their displays more useful when the scales are arranged so that improvement in an indicator corresponds with *up* on the graph. Declining performance corresponds with *down*. This system will work regardless of where your zero point is. For instance, with customer complaints, your goal (zero) would be at the top. On the other hand, the zero for production would be at the bottom unless, of course, ceasing production is your ultimate goal.

Another good formatting technique is common scaling. When looking at a series of charts showing the same parameters across different parts of the organization, all of the charts should use the same vertical scale. Then, a quick look at the chart will show whether that department represents a large or a miniscule portion of the whole. If each graph fills the vertical space available, then the smallest department and the largest will appear, at first glance, to be identical.

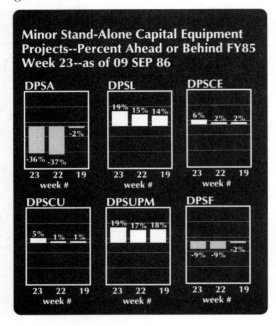

The chart to the left, from a European application, combines several bar charts to show the relative performance of several different departments. Note that the charts include both some historic background data and highlighting to show good or bad performance.

In addition, this chart illustrates well the importance of using the same scale on all charts to avoid confusing the viewer.

Do not, however, allow common scaling to interfere with communicating useful information. The scale you choose should reflect the intended goal. For example, an equitable scale for reducing payroll across a number of divisions should not be based upon the absolute number of employees in each division. With an absolute scale, the division with the largest staff would dominate the chart, regardless of its performance toward the goal.

Instead, the scale should display the percentage of divisional staff reduction to date. On this improved graph, the manager who cuts his ten-person staff by two positions justifiably will look better than the manager who cuts ten positions out of a staff of 100. Of course, if the executive wants to see the absolute number of employees, that should be included as well.

Where an aura of continuity would be useful, the EIS designers can match the types of displays that the executives are using already. For example, if the same management chartbook has been delivered for years, part of the EIS packaging can match the old format. In EIS, familiarity breeds *contentment*.

One final packaging secret: Most executives use reading glasses. EIS graphics should display indicators in a manner that is visible to the no-longer-eagle-eyed. This means avoiding a lot of small type and eschewing some of the fancier type styles and techniques. With an EIS you must get beyond the first glance. When you do, the charts should be easy to read.

Support from Above and Below

Earlier in this chapter, we noted the importance of a supportive executive sponsor. That is not the only support an EIS builder needs to succeed. Once your executive sponsor is convinced that an EIS is a worthwhile *tool for top management,* you'll need a crash course in institutional politics. In creating an EIS, you are moving into a whole new realm. The way people interact, their motivations, aspirations, and fears will be different from those you learned to deal with in the data center. All too often, when a technical specialist or "techie" gets the go-ahead to develop an EIS, the focus is on the technical aspects of the effort. This is understandable, because technology is what the technically sophisticated are most comfortable with. But it won't work.

An EIS is not just hardware and software. Even more important than building the system is selling it, and yourself, to the people who will depend upon the EIS and the people upon whom the EIS will depend. Because of its management-level visibility, many key players who have ignored other information system efforts cannot ignore an EIS. At first, some will greet the effort with skepticism and hostility. How you present the system, and how others present it, will determine both its acceptance and the level of cooperation you can expect. Present the executive information system effort to the organization in *the most nonthreatening way possible.* While there is no simple formula, over the years we've learned a few techniques that work.

Entice the Information Suppliers

Early on you need to work with the financial and managerial staff, who now create reports for executives, and the computer people, who write the programs that produce those reports. In a later chapter, we show how to involve the department managers in the process by creating a partial EIS for them. But how to involve the staff? They are key sources of information. You need them.

Demonstrate the *technological wonder* of EIS capabilities. Introduce them to some of the most impressive capabilities of the system. Maintain high visibility with the information suppliers so that they will come to you with ideas and suggestions. After all, these are the people who know the data best. But keep a low profile at the executive level while informing the lower echelons (see Chapter Five).

If the EIS is to be on-line, arrange a demonstration using the same tools that it will employ. If the output of your EIS is mainly paper, show them pocket chartbooks based on the capabilities you expect of the finished system. Good examples of both should be available from EIS vendors. Give the information suppliers a clear idea of what the end products are to be, and they can help in getting what you need to produce those end products.

It's important not to demonstrate EIS capabilities to executives prematurely because that will raise false expectations. However, it is equally important to demonstrate such capabilities to people on the lower rungs. Raising expectations at that level will do nothing but good for your EIS. Great expectations lead to great cooperation. The sizzle displayed privately to the key staff-level people you need can help launch the effort with enthusiasm and give it forward momentum.

After demonstrating the technology to the support staff, explain the EIS in terms of a new report format in which they will deliver the data they already produce. If they accept that premise, and are attracted to the delivery system, you have some very helpful new recruits.

Detente with Second-Tier Executives

A surprising number of EIS systems die on the vine because of errors in presenting the concept to the people who work directly for your executive sponsor. One erstwhile federal EIS director was assigned the task of building an EIS by the Secretary, a member of the White House cabinet. He told her to work with his assistant secretaries. However, when the idea was presented to a meeting of the Assistant Secretaries, "They were downright hostile. The idea was dead on arrival."

Second-tier executives may see real value in an EIS to help *them* manage their jobs. At the same time, they see nothing but trouble in giving the same data to their boss. The most colorful commentaries on EIS come from second-tier executives. From the manager of a midwestern plant, "Why in hell would I want to do something as stupid as that?" From the chief financial officer of a federal agency, "The boss hasn't told me he doesn't like what I give him. If he wants something different, all he needs to do is ask me." From an army colonel, "I don't want an EIS. If I have one, the general will have it, too. He'll be in my shorts all day."

Each layer of management can see the potential benefits of EIS for itself. Each layer also can see the danger of giving the same information to superiors. Such institutional hypocrisy is the natural result of the layered-management structure of a bureaucracy. "If the boss has the same information I have," they worry, "then he'll second-guess my actions and meddle endlessly."

For this type of audience, the two modes of introducing an EIS—as technological wonder, or as a top management tool—are counterproductive. The former gets you the image of a politically naive propeller head. The latter turns an insecure audience downright paranoid.

There are two basic approaches that can make EIS palatable, if not downright attractive, to second-tier executives. The first is to build a prototype that is useful to them. The second is to give them the *release key* which permits their data to be accessed by their boss. This method may not win the second-tier executives over to your cause, but it should keep them from being alienated from the EIS or tempted to sabotage the effort.

During the presentation, remember that you are working against a very powerful motivator: self interest. The audience must be given an even more powerful motivator: the firm's future. Otherwise, they will present the senior executive with a cornucopia of reasons for scuttling the project.

Win Information Systems Support

Another group you need to brief is middle management in the information systems department who are not on the EIS project team. Many will be familiar with the concept of an EIS from a technological perspective. Some may secretly have desired to build one themselves. You are likely to encounter a measure of professional competitiveness, especially when it comes to the more technical aspects of the system.

Information systems managers feel they know a great deal about hardware and software. They do. Down the road, these people can be a source of valuable advice. They may become the technological gatekeepers who can provide access to information, or computer resources, essential to the EIS, and you need them.

The briefing for information systems managers should be done as carefully as the one for the data suppliers and the second-tier executives. The information systems briefing should be one part technology, one part application, and one part industry trends.

Begin with the trends. Show the information systems managers what they already know—that EIS is a rapidly growing part of their world. Give them some background on why EIS is catching on, and examples of effective EIS in other organizations. Most important, explain what impact the technology will have on the relationship between information systems professionals and the senior executives in the organization.

Next, discuss the application. Explain the business problem that the EIS will address. Discuss the indicators you've chosen and show some of the displays you are considering. Make it clear that you are looking for their ideas concerning indicators and displays. Get them involved. *Listen.* Whether they like it or not, the success or failure of the EIS will be viewed by top executives as indicating the quality of the entire information systems organization. They have every right to contribute.

Only when you have established your credentials as an EIS expert should you discuss the technology. This undoubtedly will be your weakest card—your audience may be more familiar with the technology, especially the technology in use or on order for your organization, than you are.

Do not expect to dazzle them. Information systems people have seen a lot of whiz-bang technology before. It comes and it goes. It's not technology that counts, but what you do with it. When you introduce the technology section, ask for their ideas about other executive delivery systems for projects they may be developing. Leave an opening to encourage them to suggest some unexpected application, such as alternative EIS delivery sites (e.g., plant floor displays).

Once you have briefed all three groups—information suppliers, second-tier managers, and information systems staff—expect requests for additional briefings. These should *not* be your highest priority. Don't let demands for additional presentations get in the way of building the EIS on time and within budget. When making additional presentations, make certain you know the audience—give the right briefing to the right group!

EIS Failed? Why?

There are a few EIS lead balloons which can sink the entire project. One of the most tempting is the technological toy box. This is a portfolio of functions that look good, in theory, but are so difficult to implement that they can sink the EIS under a wave of unmet expectations. The executive calculator is a good example.

Too Many Toys

Essentially a flexible spreadsheet program, an executive calculator allows the executive to manipulate, calculate, and compare various data with little more effort than required to point at it. The executive can do analyses by pointing at a column, adding it to another column, dividing it by a value in another row, and printing the results. It can even produce an attractive graph of the results on command. Believe it or not, some demonstrations of executive calculators can make them look even better than what we've described.

Sounds great, doesn't it? Yes and no. The executive calculator may be a marvelous tool for a few executives. It can be useful in an organization with one key executive or where decisions are made by fiat, rather than by consultation or consensus. However, for most applications, such executive analysis tools are of marginal use to the executive and downright inimical to both the organization and the EIS.

The problem with executive calculators is similar to the problem of giving a spreadsheet program to executives. The executives who do use these tools create new reports and graphs. Sometimes, when all the needed data is available and the executive really understands the underlying structure and definitions of the data elements, the results can be of real value. However, far more often the calculators are applied to partial data sets about which the executives are not fully versed. The result may look good, but it is essentially garbage.

If the executive presents this result at a meeting and is subsequently embarrassed, that individual's attitude toward the EIS will be far less supportive.

This is not to say that executives needs are limited to canned reports. But, in every EIS we've seen that provided real, measurable value, the analytical displays produced for the executives were designed by experts who understood the data. The displays, both tables and graphs, offered many options. But *every type of display was pre-tested and reliable.*

Executive calculators are not the only fun feature that can cause problems. Another is instant graphics which seem flexible but won't make the charts that executives later demand. A third is the touch screen display which we have never seen an executive use except for demonstrations to visiting dignitaries.

These technological toys are fun to demonstrate, but they distract the EIS director from the key challenge—finding a business focus for the new EIS. Sometimes the toys become the reason why an EIS software package is selected. In that case, the tail is wagging the dog, and the executive soon tires of EIS toys and wants to get back to business.

Faded Sponsor Interest

Faded sponsor interest is a related problem that has undermined many EIS efforts. An executive asks for a system. A team builds one to respond to the problems identified by the executive. The executive says "thanks" and never uses the EIS. This is a knotty problem. It's as though the executive buys an expensive new car, then parks it in the garage and drives his ten-year-old bomb.

Why does this happen? For many reasons, and some of them are the right reasons. For example, new priorities may suddenly displace the old problems. A system designed to address the old, now secondary problems won't be of much use. Or there is negative organizational backlash to the EIS which causes the sponsor to keep it at arm's length. Or the technology may prove so annoying that the executive shuns the system. Or the key data delivered by the EIS may be available sooner from other sources, causing people to continue to rely on non-EIS sources.

There are dozens of reasons why a sponsor's interest may fade, and there is little that an EIS developer can do, technologically, to repair the damageother than to acquire flesible software and be prepared to refocus the efforts on new priorities. Once a sponsor has withdrawn from the EIS, it is necessary to restore that sponsor's enthusiasm or find another sponsor. In either case, the EIS developer needs to start very near the beginning to build a new EIS.

Politics

In the EIS development business, organizational politics is the leading cause of premature demise. In fact, two EIS pioneers lost their jobs in large part because of political errors made while creating and promoting their EIS systems.

Both EIS directors had similar experiences. They even bought the same EIS software package. Their first mistake was to introduce the EIS before they identified a business problem important enough to justify the cost. They gave public speeches about the EIS and provided strong endorsements for the software they had purchased. Both invested a lot of effort in gaining visibility, for their EIS and for themselves. In the process, each made some powerful enemies. Personality played a part, but it was their public visibility, and their self-promotion as the chief executives' messengers, that made them targets for jealousy. Then the executive sponsor either left or abandoned the EIS. At that point, both EIS directors realized it was the end of the road in that organization and jumped to a consulting firm. One of them summed up the lesson in four words, "Keep your head down."

Political problems can come from many directions: people whose information the EIS uses, people whose information the EIS ignores, people who do not have access to the EIS, and people who have their own firmly-held ideas about EIS.

Take the last obstacle first. People who are convinced they know more about your EIS than you do can seriously undermine your efforts via the rumor mill. Motivated as much by sour grapes as by substantive concerns, they may convince listeners that the EIS is poorly designed or seriously inadequate. This is one of the reasons why, when dealing with top executives, it is important *not* to claim more for the EIS than can be quickly delivered.

Because these nay-sayers are motivated by jealousy, the best response is to *involve* them in the EIS team. *Share* the credit with them, and share responsibility for making the system work. Give them a chance to translate their criticism into progress rather than into negativism. Where outreach cannot be done, or your critics will not cooperate, draw attention to their negative influence as early as possible. If you do, others will want to give the EIS a chance. This isolates, if only temporarily, the nay-sayers.

Another political problem is caused by people who are refused access to the EIS. These people, understandably, feel left out. Two reasons EIS developers often give for excluding people are security and cost. In fact, a successful EIS demands that information be delivered to all managers who can use it effectively.

The proper response to the problem of refused access is to *avoid* it. There is no excuse for leaving people out of the EIS loop, if they have a legitimate need to know the information. Concerns about security can be solved by giving executives access to only those parts of the EIS that each has a need to know.

The cost problem is tougher to solve, but it does have a solution. Some EIS systems require that each user buy a computer with specialty graphics, hardware, expanded memory, and enhanced software. The total for each user can exceed $15,000. The secret is to avoid this type of arrangement. The software that runs the EIS should support the computer systems you already have. If it does, then anyone who has access to a personal computer can participate in the EIS at little or no additional cost.

One often unanticipated source of opposition is people whose data the EIS *ignores.* Often long-time employees with a considerable record of service to the organization, these people may have been the miracle workers who brought computer technology into the organization. Or, they may have created the management reports currently in use. By relying on other information sources, the EIS announces the end of these peoples' usefulness.

There is no excuse for wasting such talent. These people are masters at reading and working with the data you need. Use their systems to feed the EIS. Avoid circumventing their systems to go directly to the raw data. Where possible, gather the EIS information from their existing data sets and reports. To the extent that this can be done, you have vindicated past efforts by making them part of the firm's future. Remember, some day *you* may be in the role of yesterday's whiz kid.

A good example of this approach is the monthly accounting report containing budget and actual data. Most large organizations print a huge report—to all appearances part of a hernia maintenance program. The report includes detailed data on

every account for every department. It usually shows current and
year-to-date figures, along with budget and actual data. Involve
the people who supply that data by arranging to capture the report on disk before it is printed. The disk can be read into the
EIS to update trend data delivered to the executives.

Using this approach, when the EIS delivers a number, the accountants who use the detailed report can be certain that it
matches their number. After all, the EIS data comes directly from
their source. They also will have some confidence that they know
what questions to expect from top management.

At times, some of their data really is useless to the EIS, because
it is duplicative or the executives don't want it. Then, you need
to be at your diplomatic best. Deflect the issue by asking the
sources to help you define better ways to present the data that
you are going to use.

The opposite type of problem comes from the people whose
data the system requires. Welcome to "the politics of data." Often middle managers build their professional security, and personal self-image, by being the executives' only source of key
pieces of data. If an EIS allows the executive direct access to the
data, without going through these middle managers, they are
threatened. If enough middle managers are threatened, they can
join forces and destroy an EIS.

The problem of data ownership often is not as serious as it first
appears, especially if you try to adopt the following strategy.
Leave the ownership of, and control over, the data with the current owner. Characterize your EIS as simply a conduit that will
convey the data from its current owner to the target executive(s)
and the owner retains the right to decide when to release the
data to the executives. In essence, the EIS merely re-packages
the data and data ownership remains where it is—with the middle
manager.

Throughout this course of events, keep an eye on the ultimate
goal: An EIS that becomes an indispensable tool to senior management for solving one or a few key business problems. Focus
on this goal, and many of the barriers you encounter will disap-
pear. For example, if you look closely enough at a bit of data that
seems impossible to obtain, you may find that it is unnecessary.
Or, you may find another source.

Building an EIS is a bit like finding your way through a maze
of one-way doors. Some open in. Others open out. Still others

are locked tight and won't budge. The secret is to identify which is which, as quickly as possible. It's a waste of effort to push on a door that would open with a little pull. And, it's embarrassing.

Techno-hypnosis

Beware EIS vendors who give great demonstrations. With the touch of a finger on a screen a new image appears as if by magic. Another touch causes a graph to appear, another calls an external news service, another creates instant spreadsheets, and another conjures up data on the competition. It's a fascinating demonstration. It's designed to lull you into signing a contract.

Before going into a vendor demonstration, every EIS director should watch the movie *Dracula*. Despite his unusual culinary habits, The Count was a charming fellow. At his best, he didn't overpower his victims: he hypnotized them into submission. Now you're in the right state of mind to deal with EIS systems vendors. A sprig of garlic in your lapel can't hurt.

The secret of choosing the EIS system that's right for your application is to remind yourself that you are shopping for a solution to a business problem and not a sexy technological toy. It's easy to spot an EIS director who has become a techno-hypnotic. Ask what business problem the system will solve and you'll hear that the database is newly installed and there hasn't been time to hook up the workstations. Ask what the sponsor thinks of the prototype and these folks will wax poetic about how well the vendor's demonstration was received.

See the problem? When techno-hypnotized, a person loses track of the rationale for building an EIS in the first place. All of their energies are directed toward the tools and trinkets. They've forgotten why they are there.

If the techno-hypnotic director isn't grabbed by the lapels and shaken out of the trance, the EIS could well go off on an expensive tangent and sour the corporate executives on executive information systems for years to come.

Tunnel vision

Even the best EIS directors can get preoccupied by day-to-day problems and stray off course. It is easy to get bogged down in the details: exterminating a communications bug, isolating a data problem or ensuring optimal access to a particular database. Solving these problems is important. Even more important, however, is keeping the ultimate goal foremost in mind and ensuring that sufficient time is spent on its pursuit.

The cure for tunnel vision is to keep a wider focus on making the EIS useful to senior management to solve real business problems. The executive will understand if a graph isn't available or a data file only partially so. The EIS should deliver what it can, and keep delivering. The EIS developer shouldn't wait until every feature is absolutely perfect. Gather the parts that work and show them to the executive. The effort to fix a particular problem may not be necessary after all—the executive may be satisfied with what can be delivered or may want something else entirely.

Numerophilia

Having gotten a taste of how wonderfully useful numbers can be, be careful not to get so preoccupied with the numbers themselves that you lose sight of what they stand for. Like the cobra slowly swaying to the rythm of the flute, numerophiles can see only numbers. What's beyond or behind them no longer matters.

Just because data is available on a subject doesn't mean that it should be used in an EIS. The available data may be only part of the picture and may not accurately reflect the real world. Just because information is power doesn't mean that unlimited data is omnipotence. In EIS development it is important to take care to measure the actual indicator—not an inadequate surrogate. For example, if the goal is to improve the computer's responsiveness to clients who dial in, then it is not enough to measure the computer's internal response time. The EIS must be able to determine how long the transmission network delayed the message. Otherwise the executives will be swatting flies when the real problem is a charging bull.

Data Perfectionism

On the other hand, many EIS efforts directed by senior people from a management information systems background founder because the EIS cum MIS director determines that no data can be delivered "until we get our data base in order." Most data bases are scheduled to be in order shortly after hell freezes over.

There is always a temptation to use EIS development as an excuse to obtain the support necessary to complete other information systems. People will want to use the EIS as a beast of burden and load it up with their favorite priority projects—arguing that each project is a prerequisite for developing the EIS. Remember that, at least at the outset, an EIS is built for speed and flexibility, not for carrying baggage. It is a racehorse, not a pack mule.

In some cases, executive-level interest in the EIS is perceived as useful to accelerate a wholesale effort toward a corporate data base. As valuable as the corporate data base may be for other reasons, efforts toward its development are counter-productive for executive information systems. Most of the business problems EIS can solve use only a small portion of corporate data. Reorganizing and normalizing the entire database to help feed an EIS is like repaving an airport runway in order to land a helicopter. The job may be useful, but while waiting for it to be finished, your chopper will run out of gas.

Hardware in the Arteries

Overbuying hardware and underbuying software are extremely common hazards. When first planning an EIS, most developers think the system will be used only by a few executives. If it is a good system, however, the number of users can grow by a factor of ten or more.

If the original design limits users to those who have expensive, advanced personal computers, then the design has handicapped efforts to expand the system. For the system to grow requires additional money. Therefore, when designing a personal computer-dependent system, make certain that the EIS can provide output through whatever is already available at the company and/or through cheaper personal computers. At a minimum, make it easy for future users to get paper output from the EIS. Otherwise you've hobbled your racehorse.

When planning an EIS, don't skimp on software, especially in the area of graphics display. Initial efforts to please an executive often emphasize user flexibility and "what if" programming at the cost of effective display or analytical capabilities. Down the road, however, the executive will not respond well when told that the system, bought for its flexibility, cannot prepare a particular chart a particular way.

Skimp on software, and the EIS may lose the ability to create the sophisticated boardroom-quality graphics that will help the executive bring others into the managerial process. Such a system will have brought the executive to, but not over, the brink of success. It's like snatching defeat from the jaws of victory.

4 Team EIS:
Up Close and Personal

Successful EIS systems don't just happen. They are created by a group of talented people who are different from those around them. Every installation requires a range of skills, experience, and motivation among those involved. In smaller applications, this range of talent can be vested in just a few people. More ambitious efforts will require a greater number, and diversity, of team members. The larger the team, the greater the specialization of its members in specific aspects of EIS implementation.

Each member of the team has an independent role and unique personality. In successful EIS systems, however, all team members have one characteristic in common: Successful EIS people will not allow the system to fail. Whatever it takes to make it work, they provide. They may grumble. They may demand recognition and expect financial reward, but they will stay the course. Based on our experience, a successful EIS implementation depends upon team members who will use every legal device to make the EIS work.

This dedication to duty can, and often does, ruffle bureaucratic feathers outside of the EIS team. A key role of top management in successful EIS implementation is to keep this level of feather ruffling below the threshold which could sabotage the EIS effort.

An EIS team is dynamic. It can range from a few people, each playing several roles, to a dozen or more full-time employees. The number of people an EIS needs grows rapidly after the effort is launched. The team must test many new formats, and glue together countless data sets. Personnel requirements may diminish as the system enters the long phase of continuing evolution.

Who are the key people to develop and operate a successful EIS? To identify the people, start by investigating the roles which must be played. In generic terms, this the EIS cast of characters:

Sponsor. The executive who spearheads the EIS. The sponsor identifies the business objectives the EIS will address.

Driver. The person who visualizes and pushes the EIS ahead. The driver need not be technically oriented, but must be positioned to help resolve political conflicts, secure the right people, and get the bills paid. In many cases, the sponsor and the driver are the same individual.

Devout. Dedicated to success, the devout organizes the EIS and coordinates the people who must work together to make the EIS work. This person is usually the EIS director.

Guru. With or without saffron robe, the guru is technically sophisticated and highly skilled. A guru solves the knotty technical problems and keeps an EIS functioning smoothly.

Keeper. These folks care for the data and the programs. The keepers make certain that the information which *should* be in the EIS *is* in the EIS in the necessary format. Keepers write and run programs for data analysis and graphics to shape the EIS displays. They monitor loading the data and updating the programs.

Of the five personalities that make an EIS work, sponsor, devout, driver, guru, and keeper, the role of the top management sponsor is so important that we devote much of Chapter Five to that role. You will see these other four roles and personalities reappear, in different characters, in the profiles below.

You will recognize them later when you encounter them on your path to an EIS. As you read through the profiles, be aware that you don't need to find all these people within your organization. Some may be consultants.

From time to time, a single person may play more than one role. You yourself may think that you can fill more than one role. The history of EIS implementation indicates that playing multiple roles is possible, but it doesn't make for a strong start. In the early stages of developing an EIS, each player has such a significant part to play that he or she must normally devote full attention to the task. If one person is responsible for too much, something, inevitably, will invariably slip. And that could bring the entire EIS down with it. As the EIS matures, some of the roles will become less burdensome. Then your team members can begin to assume multiple roles and perform them well. The exception to this is the role of the driver/sponsor.

The Driver

Depending upon the size of your organization, the driver may also be the only, or one of several, sponsors of the EIS. In fact, in some of the most successful EIS implementations, sponsor and driver were the same person.

Drivers are the type of people whose vocabulary seems to lack words like *no* and *can't.* A driver perceives technology as a solution to a business need rather than as an end in itself. Drivers are responsible for meeting important organizational goals; they believe that information is an essential source of power to accomplish those goals. The best drivers are enormously loyal to the people who help them to succeed. They use any opportunity to make certain that important people know how successful the EIS work was and who did it.

Meet some drivers. The year is 1978. The treasurer of a multi-billion dollar company assigns two of his employees and a team of consultants the task of developing a new on-line executive information system. The treasurer wants a system to automate access to detailed data, and to present that data in graphs. He also expects the EIS to produce displays and visuals for important board meetings.

The task was ambitious, and it led the team into uncharted territory. The EIS team members were justifiably concerned, and it showed. As they were about to leave their initial meeting, the treasurer noticed the worried look on the consultant's face. Turning to the consultant, he said, "Don't worry about this system much. Nothing will happen to *you* if it doesn't work. But you see those two other fellows?" he asked, indicating his two employees. "If it doesn't work, they're both out of here." An inspirational talk, to say the least. This driver, who was also the EIS sponsor, was far more supportive than his threat implied. He cleared away hurdles—both economic and political—to help ensure the project's success.

The treasurer was one of the most forthright executives who ever drove an EIS into an organization. But he is not unique. One government CEO dumped the organization's management information computer listings into a waste basket in front of his entire executive staff. Even with this dramatic gesture, his point was not well taken. The following month, the updated version of the computer listing was delivered to him in the same ponderous (and useless) form. Immediately, he called his personnel director and told her to transfer the responsible people to a field office "as far from headquarters as legally possible." This finally got the organization's attention. They listened attentively while he described the executive information system he wanted. With his active support and encouragement, they built it.

Another early devotee of effective EIS applications is political heavyweight Don Regan. In 1981, Regan arrived in Washington to take the helm at the U.S. Treasury Department. One of his first questions was, "Where's my EIS?" In his earlier position with Merrill Lynch, Regan had grown to rely on an EIS. He wanted one at Treasury, and he got it. A few years later when he moved to the White House, Regan requested that the Treasury provide access to his EIS in his new office as well.

Drivers can appear to be far more gentle and less demanding than the people in these examples, but their determined character surfaces when they confront something or someone standing in their path. One soft-spoken gentleman, controller of a division of a major oil company, was frustrated by the inability of his people to transfer quickly the EIS charts from an IBM mainframe to an IBM PC's. He wanted to use the EIS for boardroom presentations, and for information retrieval for individual executives. He needed the quality and consistency of mainframe graphics, along with the speed and convenience of a personal computer.

After working for several weeks with his own people trying to resolve inconsistencies between IBM mainframe and personal computers, with no results, the frustration got to him. He called his contact at IBM directly and demanded that they "Fix the problem or we'll use...." IBM fixed their internecine problem. Today mainframe charts appear on executive personal computers in less than two seconds.

The Devout

The devout is the person who believes in the driver's vision and has the organizational, technical, and management skills needed to realize that vision. The devout not only believes in the project as a loyal assistant of the driver, but also as a dedicated employee of the organization. *The ideal EIS director is also a devout.*

Devouts share another characteristic. They are excited about their role in the organization, about what they do, about what they can do, and about their career. Some view EIS as a means to gain the attention of top management, to demonstrate their competence in an important area, and, perhaps, to move up through the organization more rapidly.

Devouts are the backbone of every organization. They arrive early and leave late. They say "yes" when a job is difficult; they say "probably" when a job seems impossible. They meet their commitments. Many devouts are not fully appreciated within their organizations. The combination of exceptional ability and enthusiasm, together with the frustration that stems from lack of recognition, makes the devout EIS director a mighty weapon when unleashed by the driver.

An excellent example of a prototypical devout worked at a large midwestern bank. As is so often the case, the firm's management was a "men's club." One of the men on the executive committee assigned a woman the task of building an EIS. The target was quality: the EIS was to measure every indicator of quality that the firm's clients felt was important.

The new EIS director was a true devout. She built a system that collected data on hundreds of quality and performance indicators each week. Her EIS charted the data against clear standards of performance. She created an attractive, regularly updated book that displayed the indicators (and the EIS) to the institution's clients.

The work was burdensome. It routinely required long nights and weekends. The job was also vexatious—both technical hurdles and people within the organization blocked, rather than cleared, the way for the system. But, with the help of her EIS driver, she prevailed. Four years after launching the system, she points proudly to a system ultimately responsible for saving more than $5 million annually. In addition, her EIS has become one of the institution's most potent sales weapons. Their competition scrambled to develop their own systems. Not surprisingly, she also has become something of a folk heroine in her profession.

Another devout worked as information center director at a large electrical products manufacturer. He had ridden the information center wave as far as it would go, and felt that he was still unrecognized by top management. When presented with the opportunity to build an executive information system for the top executives, he seized it. He continued to run the information center while he built the EIS. For three months, he was constantly working with it, creating prototype after prototype until the capabilities of the system matched the needs of the executives. When his EIS became operational, his executive sponsor asked him to run it full time. He was promoted to EIS director, given a sizeable raise, and accorded the appreciation and visibility that had long eluded his best efforts.

The two people described above had little in common, in terms of their professional backgrounds. One was a computer expert; the other was not. One had run a department; the other had little management experience. Despite these differences, both were successful in building computer-based EIS systems.

From such diversity, you might infer that the EIS field is the new land of opportunity where anyone with energy and a desire for recognition can succeed. Guess again. The real world of EIS has as many thorns as it has flowers.

In one aerospace firm, the first person chosen to direct EIS development was such a loose cannon that he became a corporate-wide liability. (The hazard of a loose cannon, by the way, is not that it could go off. The real danger is that it weighs a few thousand pounds and will crush anything in its path.) In this firm, the EIS driver breathed a sigh of relief when the EIS director decided to move to another company.

"He was a paranoid," recalled the driver, a few months after the misfit left. "He took personally any criticism of the system. I couldn't clean up after him. He tore down fences faster than I could mend them. In front of everybody, he talked about how 'stupid' other people were—people whose help we had to have for the EIS to work. He made it impossible for others to work with us. Granted, he was a hard worker, but he had a much higher opinion of himself than he deserved. He was just a mid-level technical person who should never have been given the position. Picking him to head the EIS effort was the worst personnel mistake I ever made."

That he was "just a mid-level technical person" was not what stopped him from succeeding. Several of the best EIS directors were junior programmer/analysts when they started. In truth, the characteristic that damned the misfit to failure was his compulsion to place blame for problems rather than to solve them. It is common for technical people to have n us-against-them attitude toward users and toward other technical people outside their immediate domain. Technical expertise in one program or system leads some people to a near-religious conviction that their program or system is unquestionably the best. Be wary of using those people; you may rue the day they joined your team.

A mind is a terrible thing when closed.

The Guru

An EIS guru has a special talent for making others look, and feel, good. Gurus solve the the data access problems, the communications problems, and the software integration problems. Several gurus may serve an EIS project, each providing intense help in solving a related series of technical problems. While the devout may worry all night, the guru works until dawn.

One can imagine the typical EIS guru, sitting cross-legged on some cloud-shrouded mountaintop, enraptured by reading the latest manual (including appendices) on a new piece of hardware or software.

A guru has a long memory. Long enough to integrate new technical information with hard-earned experience and create novel solutions to complex problems.

A guru is easy to spot. Just look for the person to whom everyone goes for answers to technical questions. Gurus have a special characteristic that separates them from other technically competent people: they take pleasure in sharing what they know. In other words, they are *givers* rather than takers. They are also smart, very, very smart.

We illustrate with a tale of two gurus. Graduates of respected foreign academies, each majored in computer science. While attending graduate school in the U.S., they were hired as part-time research associates by a savvy EIS director. Using only an off-the-shelf software package for a personal computer, these two created an EIS that was the pride of the organization.

Their contribution to the EIS was critical. Every time the store-bought software package couldn't do something, they assembled a bridge over the problem. Officers of the software company that supplied the original package just shook their heads when discussing the gurus' work and used words like "amazing" and "incredible."

Another guru who has created, influenced, or repaired several EIS systems was a guru in the classical sense of the word. A software educator by profession, he never allowed his students to fail. He stuck with them for months after they had attended his classes, always making himself available to answer questions and help debug programs. Finally, he decided to leave the software company for which he worked to become a consultant. His reputation preceded him. Companies lined up to buy his time.

Gurus often comes in to solve a single problem or a set of problems and then fade out of the project. It can be dangerous to keep gurus on an EIS project after they have solved the problems in which they specialize. With boundless energy and generos advice, gurus tend to get involved in problems far afield of their original mandate. As their expertise becomes less critical, they may encroach upon the EIS director's managerial prerogatives.

Gurus, as a class, are better at managing themselves than they are at managing other people. Their communications skills may leave something to be desired. Put gurus in charge of an EIS project and they may try to do the entire job alone. They seem to forget that, to succeed, even the Lone Ranger needed help from Tonto now and then.

Related to the guru, but not quite at the guru level of achievement, is the journeyman developer. These are computer jockeys who get the job done through hard work and persistence, rather than magic. Where the guru can walk on water, the journeyman developer will throw stones into the creek until a bridge is built. When you can't find a guru, a journeyman developer should get the job done, but you'll need a little more time.

The Keepers

There are two types of keepers: software keepers maintain EIS programs, and data keepers maintain the information. Keepers do the everyday tasks necessary to keep the EIS data up to date. At times, data keepers monitor computer-based data loading; at other times, they enter the EIS data.

Data keepers may work for the EIS director or they may be part of the information owner's staff. In some cases, all of the data to be fed into the EIS may be provided by the same staff who have traditionally been responsible for keeping top management informed.

Often the software keeper needs to synthesize information coming from other systems and to translate it into a form which is digestible by the EIS. After the guru leaves the project, some organizations rely on their keepers to modify report and graph formats as needed. This latter function can be very important to the vitality of the entire EIS.

The keeper represents an interesting—and somewhat contradictory—mix of characteristics. On one hand, a keeper is inherently detail-oriented, perfectly at ease spending long hours ferreting the right bit of data out of reams of sources. This tends to be the type of task that a "loner" enjoys. On the other hand, the keeper must be gregarious enough to cooperate with the other EIS team members and adapt to changes.

The little details mean a lot to the keeper. Keepers know what a forest looks like, but they are more interested in studying individual trees. Because they want to know the details, it is important that the EIS director explain to each keeper exactly why what the keeper is doing is crucial to the success of the entire system. More important, the keeper should understand the central role of the EIS in the functioning of the organization and the achievement of mutual goals.

The story of one special keeper illustrates most of these points. She had worked in business planning, sales, and information systems before taking on the job of daily support of the EIS's news service. Her job was to monitor external news services, identify the items of critical interest to her company, and enter them into the EIS. Her job started before sunrise, monitoring news from Europe. It ended late in the evening, as news sources followed the sun westward . When asked about her value to the organization, the executive who runs the department that built the EIS said, "She's our eyes and ears on the world."

Of course, most EIS keepers do not have the breadth of responsibility of the woman described above. But it is not uncommon to hear words like "essential" used to characterize them and their activities. The good ones work carefully but quickly. While others stand around discussing what to do, they are doing it.

Secretaries are often chosen to be EIS data keepers. This seems natural, since secretaries always have had a key role in providing information to their executives. Effective secretaries know each of the players who supply the data. They also know corporate politics and how best to ensure that the right information gets into the system without a lot of ruffled feathers or bruised egos.

An ambitious secretary can also be an excellent choice for software keeper—adjusting the EIS programs to incorporate changes in report or graph formats. They respond to the challenge by enthusiastically attending training classes and reading the EIS manuals. Because they want to learn, they are not afraid to ask questions or call for help.

Keepers sometimes work alone; more often they are part of a team that keeps the information up-to-date. One large aerospace company has four keepers. In another, there are two. The number of keepers is determined both by the amount and importance of the data that must be monitored, screened, and entered into the EIS. Where large volumes of dynamic data must be kept up-to-the-minute, many keepers may be needed. For example, in a major air defense center, nearly two hundred keepers monitor incoming data and feed the EIS displays.

The EIS Director

Most analyses of executive information systems focus on three aspects: the importance of the sponsoring executive; the software and hardware; and the economic, organizational, and political impact of the resulting systems. What those analyses miss is the critical role played by the EIS director—the man or woman who orchestrates the resources, people, politics, data, hardware, and software to create a functioning EIS. Every EIS system has a director, without whom the system would not exist.

In nearly every successful EIS, the devout emerges as the EIS director. As you read about the experiences of the people in our case studies, try to keep one insight in mind. We've met dozens of EIS directors. They are a diverse group. For every generalization that applies to them, there are a half-dozen exceptions.

One thing that they all have in common, however, is that they really like what they are doing. They profoundly believe that a good EIS can yield benefits beyond the organization itself. They are on the front lines of a revolution. If all this sounds a bit heroic, you haven't been infected by EIS yet. Just wait.

The role of EIS director is one of the finest jobs available. It offers a type of visibility that is simply unavailable from any other quarter. Many of the senior managers in the organization will come to know the EIS director, both personally and professionally. The EIS director makes their jobs easier, helps them identify key indicators, and finds data needed to track progress. The role of EIS director is a shortcut to a promotion.

The job is also good for people who like instant gratification. The EIS director's role is gratifying because of the impact of the systems and the speed with which they can be created. Where else in the information technology business can one person manage a project from concept to maturity in six months and, perhaps, save the firm a million dollars along the way?

EIS directors are a mixed breed. Some are consultants; others are employees of the organization that will use the EIS. Some come from information systems departments; others from information centers. Still others are nontechnical managers or staff. Many of them learn what computing they need as they go along. In general, EIS directors are skilled at ad libbing.

An EIS director's position may begin as a part-time activity. It can grow into a full-time position with staff. In less ambitious systems, the job of director is temporary until the system is up and running. After that, the job of maintaining the EIS may be pulled (or pushed) into a more traditional organizational unit.

However, there are downsides to the EIS director's job: Tight deadlines; Friday night changes to be operational Monday morning; data-base extraction, summarization, and graphing systems due in a few days; and equally absurd requests. If you take pleasure in doing the impossible, it's the job for you. If, on the other hand, you relish order, stability, predictability, privacy, and a forty-hour work week, keep looking.

As we said before, successful EIS directors are a diverse group with different backgrounds, skills, and tastes. Within this variety, however, there are a few things that every prospective EIS director should know before he or she takes the plunge. Look upon the following as a condensed version of two decades of touring through the wonderful world of EIS.

What EIS Directors Need to Know

To a great extent what follows is a distillation of the profiles and a summary form of more detailed information presented elsewhere in this book. We present it in shortened form here as a quick reference tool for executives who want to be forearmed in preparation for a meeting with someone who is proposing an EIS. In addition, for the prospective EIS developer, this section should serve as a review and check list.

About EIS

An EIS is a support system for executives. That's all you really *must* remember. It helps executives do what they already have been doing by making the task easier or faster. Sometimes it helps by giving them a way to do new tasks that are needed as the organization changes. Building a successful EIS requires understanding exactly what executives do and where an EIS can help. Fit the EIS to the reality of modern management, not vice versa.

In rare instances, an EIS can be a computer system that feeds corporate data to executives and allows them to wander through the data and conduct their analyses at will. More often, the EIS delivers pre-packaged answers—in the form of charts and data tables—to questions that arise during the day. This typical system is complemented by a two-way communications system that opens powerful channels between executive and organization.

In many EIS systems, the executive does not run the EIS directly, in hands-on fashion. Instead, the system is used by aides, executive secretaries, and the people who provide management briefings. From that perspective, an EIS supports what the executive does, rather than supporting the executive directly. An EIS located behind the scenes on the executive secretary's desk and in the executive conference room is just as important as one sited center stage on the executive's desk.

What supports the throne is as important as who sits on it.

About the Organization

Recognizing the indicators that tell when the organization is ready for EIS is a valuable talent that can help ensure that the system will be worth its cost. Each organization, and even each major component within an organization, becomes aware of the need for EIS at different times and, often, in different ways. In successfully implementing an EIS, timing is of the essence. Move too early and you can outdistance your lines of support. Move too late and somebody else will get there first.

A clear indication that an organization is ready for EIS comes when a senior executive returns from a trip and says, "I just saw (company x's) new executive information system. That looks like something we can use. Check it out." As long as that executive is high enough in the organization, such comments are sufficient to justify the next step in building an EIS.

Another excellent, if subtle, indicator of EIS readiness is the installation of a new executive whose mission is to save a sick organization or to meet an overwhelming challenge in a new way. That executive is a good candidate to sponsor an EIS. (A few graceful steps, outlined in Chapter Ten, can make an organization with a new key executive EIS-ready in short order.)

If your executives have not discovered EIS for themselves and there are no new executive stars to which you can hitch your EIS wagon, there may still be evidence that indicates that the organization may be ready for an EIS. Look for a rising tide of comments from senior executives about the lack of timely data and the problem of being "buried in paper." Executives who make these comments are potential EIS sponsors. They are not good sponsors, however, unless the organization simultaneously embarks on a major modernization program, reorganizes, or launches a major initiative. Combine executives, who are frustrated with the status quo, together with an organization that is investing in change, and you have fertile ground for planting the seeds of an EIS.

Beware of incomplete signals and false starts. For instance, the firm may have a senior information-systems executive who feels that EIS technology is ripe for exploitation and authorizes a team to explore the alternatives. You can be pretty sure that this is a false signal and that the organization isn't ready for EIS. Without a high-level executive sponsor from outside of the information-systems department, the information systems study team will produce a report scarcely worth the paper on which it's printed. The team will discuss a series of technical capabilities, give each a weight, and poll the best-known EIS vendors to determine whether or not they offer those capabilities. Then the study team will add up each vendor's weighted scores and declare a winner. And nobody will care.

These task forces and study groups are pointless if the team doesn't know who the proposed EIS will serve or what it is supposed to monitor. Such studies are the ultimate philosophical exercise lost within the ultimately pragmatic environment.

About the Systems

Software is available that will support executive information systems on most popular computer hardware: IBM mainframe, Digital VAX, Apple Macintosh, and IBM PC. EIS software offers many capabilities to support the modern executive: electronic mail, graphics, data acquisition, data analysis, calender management, telephone directories and automatic dialing, action lists, and organization charts, to name a few. They differ in many ways.

Experienced EIS directors agree on one thing: most EIS ven-

dor demonstrations create expectations that the systems themselves have great difficulty satisfying. In particular, the demonstrations imply that the firm's data can be fed into the systems
and, voila, an instant EIS. Reality intrudes.

About the Executive

The type of executive every EIS director wants as sponsor is one
who makes decisions quickly and supports the people who implement those decisions. This sponsor understands the concept of
prototyping. After each prototype review session, another meeting is scheduled to review the *next* prototype. The executive's
actions reinforce the importance of the project by giving it the
time and attention it deserves. The best executive sponsors ask
for changes freely, with little concern that the changes may take
many nights to accomplish. After all, the EIS is central to the
company's future.

Along the pathway to an EIS, you will encounter an interesting
array of executive types. Each type offers an intriguing mix of
promise and peril. Here are a few, and some advice on what to
do when you encounter one as executive sponsor or driver.

The hands-off delegator is a tough challenge. He or she tells
an aide that the EIS should go forward and, "Don't bother me
until it's ready." The aide then becomes the driver. All the EIS
director can do is hope and pray that the aide really knows what
the sponsor needs. If the aide is wrong, the EIS director will pay
the piper. Most aides are too preoccupied with their own careers
to stand behind decisions made during EIS development.

For example, a few years ago in the Pentagon, a general ordered a colonel to create an EIS to automate the briefing room
Ignoring the objections of the EIS director, the colonel installed
a phalanx of high-tech display equipment in the briefing room.

When the general arrived to see the new briefing room in all
its glory, he couldn't read the displays. His eyesight wasn't great
and the display wasn't bright enough. The general candidly
asked, "What's this crap?" Sensing the change in atmosphere,
the colonel quickly covered his behind with, "I told (the EIS director) it wouldn't work. We'll get it fixed right away, sir." The
EIS was shifted to 35mm slides, and the EIS director's hide was
saved only by the colonel's reassignment a continent away.

An executive sponsor to avoid at all costs is one who knows
technology and sees the EIS project *not* as a means to solve a busi-

ness problem but as a search for the technological equivalent of the Holy Grail. For example, a second-level government executive with extensive experience in information processing became an EIS driver. The agency head served as EIS sponsor. The sponsor asked for an EIS to "change the way we run this organization and give new visibility to high priorities."

The EIS driver responded by purchasing hundreds of thousands of dollars worth of EIS software and time sharing. He gave the system a snappy name and, at the urging of his EIS software vendor, he started promoting the system shamelessly. Despite the expenditure of more than $2 million in taxpayers' money, the EIS did little more than deliver copies of existing monthly reports and news articles. It clearly did not improve productivity.

When the sponsor left, the driver was out, too. Unfortunately, the staff and consultants who diligently tried to follow this driver's direction had their reputations sullied in the process.

About Consultants

Due to the varying level of personnel needed and the technical training required, an EIS development application can benefit from a judicious use of consultant talent. Consultants can contribute in five key areas. First, they can help to create working prototypes very quickly, when they are most needed—very early in the game. The experience consultants bring from comparable tasks in other firms is seldom available in-house.

Second, consultants provide extra hands (and minds) to build the initial formats and weave together data from various sources. Because they've done it before, consultants often perform these tasks much more quickly than in-house staff. It is crucial, however, that the consultants you use be versed fully in the hardware and software you're using. If not, you'll be paying for a pretty expensive learning curve.

Third, consultants offer technical gurus—those rare magicians who can make the personal computers talk to the mainframe and integrate the graphics, electronic mail, and other components. Using consultants to provide your guru is often a wise move, and can be a *very* wise move.

Fourth, consultants can help define the business problems that the EIS will solve, although we have seen many cases where consultant-supplied business problem analyses were useless. One of the easiest times to start an EIS is after a top-flight consulting firm has assisted the chief executive (or other EIS sponsor) in creating a strategic plan. Within the pages of that plan may lie opportunities for EIS.

Fifth, the consultants can assist management information staff in understanding the business objectives, in deciding which indicators are most appropriate, and in incorporating the system into the organization. This should be done with caution. We've seen any number of EIS directors wounded by consultants who didn't understand the business.

Consultants are not a prerequisite of a successful EIS. In fact, many systems have been built without them. Some of the greatest waste in the history of EIS developments has resulted from an uncertain client giving a consultant broad discretion. A consultant can invest many (expensive) hours in exhaustive assessments of needs, options, and recommendations. Such contracts can exceed $100,000. The price tag is seldom justified by the results.

If the job can be done in-house, the firm will save both time and money. If outside help is needed, consultants are best used to provide a very concentrated combination of needs assessment and prototyping. Assuming you have selected a consulting team that both understands the business and can build prototypes rapidly, this type of approach can be a short-cut to a working system.

There are more than a half-dozen good EIS consulting firms which can provide the services described above. The best, if not the only, way to find one which will suit your needs is to contact satisfied clients. When in doubt, contact people with acknowledged expertise in EIS. Their advice should be reliable since their reputation is built upon it.

5 Involving the Executive: Of Goals and Godfathers

An executive information system serves no purpose if it doesn't meet the *real* objectives of its client executives. How is it possible to pursue those objectives without clear consultation with the executives themselves? Building an EIS without a sponsoring executive is like jumping out of a plane without a parachute— exhilarating, short-lived, and the ultimate impact may be quite unpleasant.

Don't build an EIS and then search for an executive to use it. On the other hand, some cynical second-tier executives claim that it is difficult to interest an executive in any new project that is not completed already. They would argue that people who have the power to authorize a project often want to see what they're buying before they'll sign the check. As a result, one may be tempted to buy or build an EIS in hopes that executives will like what they see and start using it.

The prospective EIS developer should avoid this temptation.

Finding a Sponsor

As the benefits of modern executive information systems become known, more and more executives are nominating themselves as EIS sponsors. They take the initiative and demand better information from the head of the information services department or an assistant. They want information that is more timely, more consistent, more distilled, or they just want more information.

One of the most important lessons for an EIS developer to learn is that the executive client doesn't need to understand what an EIS is in order to want one. Nor does he need to understand sophisticated concepts to make good use of a sophisticated computer. While it's important to explain to the executive *what* an EIS can do, it may be even more important to *avoid* trying to explain *how* the EIS will do it! If you forget this rule you may find yourself expounding on a "relational database access routine" to your sponsor. That glazed-over look on the executive's face should be your clue to change the subject and return to common English usage.

Some executives will know the term executive information system, and will ask for one by name. Do not confuse use of the term with a thorough understanding of EIS. The only prudent approach is to assume the executive simply wants better information and is using a familiar term. In fact, it is sometimes wise to eschew the term EIS entirely and name the system after the business objective it is designed to meet. For example, call it a quality information system, a competitive analysis system, or a sales information system. A more descriptive name makes it easy for the sponsor and other executives to support the effort.

Creating a Demand

Cultivating executive interest should be done with care. If no executive comes to you looking for help, and you want to build an EIS, then you will need to create a demand for such a system.

The first step, of course, is to identify the executive most likely, and/or most appropriate, to sponsor the EIS. Look for an individual with as many of the following attributes as possible.

Authority: Able to authorize both the EIS effort and the resources necessary.

Influence: Looked up to as a leader because of his position in the firm, or as a pioneer based on prior success in using advanced methods.

Attitude: Views technology as a tool for achieving a goal rather than as a curiosity to explore.

Management style: Gives credit to subordinates where it is due, and helps subordinates to navigate the political quagmire.

With luck, you will find all of these characteristics in one person. More likely, you'll need to trade off one attribute against another to identify the best candidate.

Relying on the wrong sponsor is one of the most common elements among failed EIS projects. For example, management information systems executives often make weak EIS sponsors. This is not due to any personality defect on their part, but because they hail from a part of the organization, information systems, that is viewed by other executives as an internal support function. If the EIS is designed to serve the MIS executive as its ultimate user, it can be a big success. The problem arises when the MIS executive is sponsoring the EIS as a proposal for use by other executives in the organization. The influence of an MIS executive is rarely strong enough to make the executive information system seem relevant to more line-oriented managers.

Once you've identified a prospective sponsor, the next step is to arrange a meeting. There are many ways of presenting information to whet executive interest in an EIS. One that we find effective is to send the executive copies of relevant articles from respected publications such as *Business Week* (June 27, 1988), *The Wall Street Journal* (June 20, 1988), *The New York Times* (August 21, 1988), or *Fortune* (March 13, 1989). Or send copies of articles about EIS use in your industry, or in an industry with goals and problems similar to yours. Send them to the target executive(s) with a note saying, "We would like to discuss how this can work here. If you are interested, please let me know." Include your phone number.

In a week or so, if you've had no response then set up a meeting with the executive's special assistant. Show the articles, explain what could be done for the boss, and ask to discuss the idea of an EIS with the executive.

If these actions don't work, then the timing is wrong, the choice of executive is wrong, or you are the wrong person.

It's tempting to ask a superior to intercede with the senior executive on behalf of your EIS. While this approach seems reasonable, it is seldom advisable. For an EIS to work, trust is of the essence. The sponsoring executive will depend on you to create a system to serve executive-level needs. Whether the EIS effort succeeds or fails, don't forget one key factor in the timing of executive information systems—the PDL effect. PDL is pure dumb luck, and it will surely influence the chances of the EIS initiative being in the right place at the right time.

Choosing a Business Objective

One important lesson technologists learn about EIS is that its purpose is *not* merely to provide information to an executive. Its purpose is to provide the information the executive *needs* and/or *wants* to meet selected goals.

Why would a very busy executive take a lot of time to work with you to shape an EIS? The only correct answer to this question is "because it helps solve an immediate problem." Whether or not the information system helps meet long-term goals, it must solve an immediate problem in order to merit the executive's attention. Look at it from the executive's perspective: there are twenty or more people banging on the door asking for time. Every one of their needs creates a current problem for the executive.

To the busy executive an EIS can look a lot like a time-consuming technology toy—unless it's relevant to the organization's immediate problems. If it's not clear how an EIS can contribute to the resolution of an immediate problem, or meet an immediate goal, the executive will not have time for it.

Try a little investigatory work before the first meeting with a potential sponsor. Get copies of the executive's recent speeches. Look through the company newsletter for indications of the executive's and the organization's priorities. Check the reading file or the annual plan. Finally, talk with people who work closely with the executive to learn which issues can either inspire your sponsor to superlatives—or evoke expletives.

The initial meeting to solicit the executive's sponsorship should be a well-orchestrated event. Three things should happen: First, the executive is briefed on EIS, placing special emphasis on what it can do within that particular organization. Second, a sample EIS application demonstrates that these systems represent a quantum leap beyond the traditional management information systems. Remember that this does not mean building an entire EIS—only a small exemplary demonstration using relevant corporate detail. Third, an interactive discussion ensues regarding the business objectives that an EIS could help the executive achieve.

The following section provides some ideas for an EIS briefing and demonstration. By the time you finish this book, you'll be armed with the knowledge you need to produce an effective briefing of your own.

To start with, try to include a few key elements in your briefing. The first is visual proof that you understand the problem from the executive's perspective. To demonstrate this, you might lift a copy of the weighty management reports currently produced and point out how difficult and inefficient it is to find key information.

Next, present your own definition of an EIS. Focus on the uses of an EIS to help solve business problems. Depict the system as an active tool rather than a passive information resource. The executive's meter is running, so don't get bogged down in the details of how an EIS will work. The more time you take explaining, the less time you'll have to sell the concept and identify some target business problems.

The whole idea behind EIS is to make information flow efficiently. Your presentation should embody this concept and be a testimonial to effective executive-level communication. As Marshall McLuhan is often misquoted as having written, "The medium is the message."

Stimulate the competitive spirit by discussing concrete examples of EIS solving problems that are likely to be of interest to your executive audience. Use your library, or your connections, to obtain actual or realistic copies of the displays from similar EIS operations elsewhere. If there are none, or if they are more carefully guarded than the formula for Coca-Cola, use the examples in this book to fill the gap.

Many executives are a bit intimidated by, and therefore hostile to, technology they don't fully understand. You can overcome this intimidation factor by demonstrating an EIS delivery system's friendliness and ease of use. Whether on paper or on-line, this demonstration will serve as a proof of the concept.

Until shown something that looks real, many executives will react as though you were speaking Sanskrit. Show them something they will recognize—improve on the familiar. Your demonstration will be most effective if it delivers some of the information currently buried in the the firm's management reports. Surprisingly, we have found that this demonstration need not be on-line. Besides, you have only so much time to invest in preparing for the demonstration. That time could be better invested in the substance you want to convey than in fine-tuning an on-line system. Remember, if your briefing depends on an on-line finale, someone or something could prematurely pull the plug.

Perhaps just as effective as an on-line display would be a collection of pocket chartbook samples such as we show elsewhere in this book. This will give the executive something to examine closely and will make the point that needed information can be right at his fingertips.

Having made the point of how effective EIS information is, you can logically shift to a discussion of the type of business problems and real business objectives that this particular EIS should be designed to address. *Engage* the executive in discussing the special goals to be met. Along with identifying the objectives and problems that occupy the executive's time, what you really need is some sense of priority. It simply would not do to develop a prototype system to address a problem on the lowest rung of the executive's priority ladder.

Keep in mind that you want three results from this first meeting. First, gain the executive's confidence in your ability to produce without wasting the executive's time. Second, obtain the executive's authorization to develop a prototype to demonstrate how an EIS will help. Third, get agreement on one or two objectives or problems that are important enough for the prototype to help solve.

The entire meeting should be designed to take less than an hour, with the EIS presentation and demonstration taking less than half of that time. Time is valuable to the people being briefed. An appreciation of the value of executive time is demonstrated by keeping the briefing short. In the event that the briefing may be rescheduled or, more likely, shortened, be prepared. Practice a ten-minute version of the entire briefing and demonstration. Efficiency and brevity will be appreciated.

The key discovery the executive should make during the presentation is that an EIS solves business problems, and that an EIS is most effective when applied to a particular, clearly defined business objective.

Selecting the Proper Objective

While each business or government organization has its own unique needs, problems, and priorities, there are certain general patterns that many successful EIS developers have followed in defining their core objectives. Many of the most useful EIS objectives fall into one of five categories: improve responsiveness to customers or quality of product, increase efficiency, reduce costs, track project status, and ensure consistent management information. Depending on the context, almost any business objective could be a candidate for EIS, as long as it meets three criteria: it must be important, it must be influenced by executive-level monitoring, and it must be quantifiable.

The objective must be *important* enough that reaching it will be widely acknowledged. Such objectives are often client-related, such as improving customer service, improving product quality, or increasing the percentage of repeat customers. An example of an objective that isn't important enough could be "increasing employee use of gym facilities." That objective may be important to the employees and to the personnel health executive, but few would acknowledge the importance of an EIS that helped meet such an objective. A better alternative might be "reducing the cost of health insurance," or "reducing sick leave."

The objective must be influenced by *executive-level* monitoring. A sales-oriented objective that executive monitoring can impact might be "increasing the percentage of sales coming from high-profit products." An objective like "improving daily sales figures" does not meet this criterion. Sales are important, but few people would acknowledge that the EIS influenced the daily numbers.

The objective must be *quantifiable* with short-term (monthly, weekly, or daily) measurements. Consider such objectives as reducing the use of overtime, increasing the number of new clients, or reducing delays in collecting accounts receivable. Such goals will help meet larger objectives, such as improved return on investment, while also meeting all three criteria for a good EIS objective. On the other hand, a goal such as, "Improving return on investment" by itself normally would not meet these criteria. Outside of the banking industry, the measurement cycle for return on investment is generally on a quarterly basis, and too much time passes between updates for faster delivery of the information to be of much value.

In discussions with executives, elicit their perspective. Do not hinder the conversation by setting a lot of ground rules that can distract the executive from the task at hand. For example, in discussions of objectives and current business problems with the executive, don't mention the criteria outlined above. Instead, use the criteria *after* the meeting to select from among several objectives that the executive mentions. In addition, the way a problem or objective is described back to the executive should dovetail with these criteria.

The search is for one or two objectives, but that doesn't mean that the EIS can't also deliver other useful information. As explained elsewhere, the EIS can be the delivery system for news, mail, standard printed reports, and any other information. But the system will hardly be worth the investment if it does not, at a minimum, help meet key business or mission-related objectives.

Some Useful Objectives

This section offers examples of real-world objectives that have been met and business problems that have been solved using EIS. Each example is accurate and factual, based upon our own experience and direct knowledge. As they used to say on *Dragnet*, the names (and some identifying details) have been changed to protect the innocent.

We'll return to some of these examples, throughout the book, to illustrate other aspects of the EIS experience. It is our intent that some of the characters will become familiar and you will benefit from sharing their successes and their defeats.

Improve Responsiveness to Customers

Regardless of how many customers an organization has, unless it has a comfortable monopoly the firm's future depends upon responding to customer needs and preferences. In fact, customer convenience and specialized services are at the cutting edge of much corporate competition.

It is simply not true that a better mousetrap will have customers flocking to your door. To get customers you also must make it convenient and easy for the customer to replace the old mouse trap with your new one.

Example one. In 1981, a midwestern bank found that it was under extreme competitive pressure from New York and California banks. The firm's executives decided that the bank's competitive position depended on the perceived quality of its service to customers. The bank decided to improve the perception of its service by improving the service itself. Improved customer service was the main objective of an EIS developed by the bank.

During the three-month design and implementation phase, bank executives interviewed clients and their own marketing representatives to identify more than 700 indicators of the quality of customer service. These indicators ranged from timeliness of check processing and computer systems availability to the number of customer complaints. The EIS tracked each of these indicators and reported progress weekly.

Each week, top executives reviewed the indicators that their subordinates saw as critical, based upon overall priorities and indicators of good or bad performance. Within a few months, the service indicators began to improve. The result was happier customers and considerable savings (in reduced cost for correcting errors). Executives estimated that the system, which cost approximately $500,000 to develop and implement, saved approximately $4 million per year.

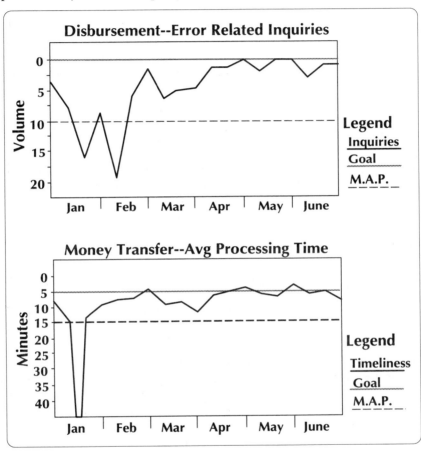

These charts show calls from clients concerned with errors and the time required to process money transfers. The charts illustrate two key characteristics of effective display of quality indicators. First, the zero level is at the top so that good is up and bad is down. Second, both the goal and the level of minimal acceptable performance are shown. The viewer can see at once if the quality indicator is good, bad, or in between. The improvement of the indicators over time is ample testimony to the effectiveness of the EIS.

Example two. The state public utilities commission denied an important rate increase to a New England utility on the grounds that it was slow and unresponsive to consumer complaints. The public utilities commission, in effect, held a rate increase hostage until the utility improved its customer service.

The utility implemented an EIS to give top management direct access to status reports on every customer complaint. Designed and operational within two months, the EIS improved organizational response by halving the time it took to settle complaints. A few months after the EIS was implemented, the public utilities commission granted the rate increase.

Example three. A major provider of systems for military aircraft was in a highly competitive environment with only a few competitors. Low bidder would win, but low bidder also had to deliver, and make a profit. What the competition could bid depended on two things: their financial strength and their accumulated backlog of orders.

Both pieces of information were available, but not in a format that provided useful input into the firm's decision-making process. In response, their marketing department created an EIS that combines an enormous amount of data on each of the competitors. The EIS has information on the competitors' backlog, financial strength, and outstanding bids. With this data, the firm can estimate how aggressive it can be with each new competition.

Improve Efficiency

Improved efficiency and increased productivity are among the most important, and most difficult to accomplish, of management goals. One of the difficulties lies in the need to define and isolate an accurate indicator of efficiency which can be influenced by management policy. Once such an indicator has been defined, implementing an executive information system to track its improvement is a logical next step.

Example one. During the last cyclical downturn in the paper industry, a large New York-based paper company faced huge carrying costs for excess inventory. This inefficient management of inventory gained the attention of top management, but nothing seemed to be happening. Memos to plant managers failed to alleviate the problem. At one point, the firm's chairman quipped that the only progress being made to reduce their inventory of paper was the amount of paper being consumed by memoranda on the subject.

Finally, the chairman ordered an EIS that monitored inventory levels in every paper storage location. In addition to weekly status reports and graphics on inventory changes and closing levels, the EIS provided the name and phone number of the person responsible for each inventory site. This level of visibility was enough to prove to the local managers that top management was serious about the inventory problem. In just three months, inventory dropped to desired levels.

The firm's chairman gives full credit for the achievement to the EIS. When the inventory goal was reached, the chairman asked the EIS director to expand the system to monitor several other goals. In a short time, the EIS director became a trusted aide of the chairman.

Example two. An eastern electric utility company operated on-line information systems providing various services to its clients. One system provided customer account information, another managed assignments of service crews, and a third controlled assignments of emergency crews. These systems suffered from ultra-slow response times, with operators waiting up to seven seconds at each individual step of the inquiry. The laggard computer frustrated operators and annoyed clients.

Top executives at the utility set a goal of reducing response time by 80 percent, and implemented an EIS to monitor progress toward the objective. EIS graphic displays updated information showing average response time each hour. The system delivered daily updates to each of the top executives. The system also produced wall-sized displays of key graphs. These were prominently displayed where the computer-performance management staff couldn't miss them. Six months after implementing the EIS, the organization reached its computer-responsiveness goal, making the staff more efficient and the clients more satisfied.

Example three. Efficiency also can be improved by restoring a competitive climate within an organization. Four years ago, a family-owned 100-store chain of clothing boutiques hired a new president to revitalize the firm. His predecessor had been lax in cost control and too tolerant of store managers who were not performing. The new president needed to be more assertive, but also wanted to be fair. He wanted to base his reviews of the store managers on objective information.

To get that information, the president authorized a $1 million project to automate the collection of sales and cost data from every store on a weekly basis. He built an EIS on this data. Using data on prior performance of the chain, he established benchmarks and compared each against other stores in similar areas. He monitored the data, made phone calls, and changed staff to reinforce the importance of performance.

Within eighteen months, the company shifted from a small loss to $2 million profit per year. During the next two years, he rapidly expanded the number of stores while maintaining close oversight. Last year, the firm's profits exceeded $8 million.

Reduce Costs

One way to reduce cost is to track expenses more carefully. Large companies can easily be victimized by unauthorized, and unexpected, changes in prices. Tens of thousands of invoices arrive every week at large firms. The accounting staff cannot check every item on every invoice against purchase orders, especially in light of frequent changes in vendor item numbers. Many increases slip by undetected. While the individual amounts are small, their cumulative effect can mean millions of dollars.

Example one. An aerospace contractor experienced creeping cost increases from its suppliers and subcontractors in which small changes to the prices were added to each bill. The firm set up an EIS to chart and highlight price changes. The EIS produced more than 10,000 charts every month. Each multi-part display showed the total costs of a component compared with the amount budgeted. Other charts showed the changes in unit cost of vendor-supplied parts.

Creeping prices were obvious immediately. The word quickly spread among the suppliers and price creep declined remarkably. Today the firm's suppliers know that if they change the price of a product, they are likely to be asked for a detailed justification of the change.

Example two. Another way to reduce costs is by examining operations more carefully. The following example demonstrates how management information system directors can sponsor EIS systems for use within their departments.

At Electronic Data Systems, running computers is a primary line function. In 1978, a senior vice president with a management information systems background installed an EIS to track costs in his data centers. The system allowed him to select any or all data centers, time periods, and cost categories. The EIS produced graphs of the revenue and spending trends and highlighted any divergence of actual from budgeted expenses.

"Before we installed the EIS, my data center managers and their staff slipped expenses through," he notes. "Once they knew that all their spending would be visible, they were far more careful to get approval in advance. We cut the growth in these costs from 18 percent last year to about ten percent this year."

Example three. Another way to reduce costs is to reduce waste associated with operations. The U. S. Government Printing Office, as we mentioned earlier, is the largest publishing house in the world. It either does, or contracts for, the printing of nearly all federal publications. That amounts to tens of thousands of titles per year! The potential for major savings from even small reductions in waste is obvious.

Three years ago, the Public Printer asked for an EIS and defined five objectives for the system to monitor. Waste reduction was high on the list. The chief executive asked his deputies to determine what indicators should be measured to ensure that waste was being reduced. Those indicators were monitored monthly and presented via graphic displays on terminals throughout the organization. Some displays were installed where the production was carried out, and the displays showed the status of performance indicators within each manager's work area. Progress toward the established goals was visible to all. Within a year, reduction goals were surpassed.

In the case of the Government Printing Office, implementation of the EIS resulted in a quiet revolution in its way of doing business. The Public Printer was justifiably proud of his people. When asked why he placed terminals on the production floor, he responded, "Because that's where the work gets done. The only people who can make changes in the quality of our products are the people who make the product. If we let them know what things are important and how they are doing on those things, then they will fix it."

One long-term GPO supervisor, jaded by years on the job, was astounded by the new EIS. "I had always known we were doing things the wrong way," he volunteered. "Until the color EIS system came in I didn't know how bad off we were. Those charts gave me the excuse to try some ideas I had been thinking about for years. You know what? They worked!"

Example four. Costs can also be cut by reducing payroll. Asian imports were putting pressure on a major consumer products company. The company's board of directors agreed that a fifteen percent reduction in staff was necessary to regain competitive advantage. To implement the reduction, the president issued a memorandum instructing all middle managers to freeze new hiring and not to replace any people who retired or left.

Earlier efforts toward the same goal largely had been ignored by middle management, and reductions had taken too long to implement. For the success of this effort, the executive created an EIS that monitored each of the firm's 300-plus cost centers. Each week, the system displayed the number of people who had left or were terminated and the number of new hires. The senior executive could monitor each manager's activities, and each manager knew that any additions to staff would be scrutinized at the highest levels. This time, the needed reductions were achieved far more quickly.

Track Project Status

An EIS can improve project management in two ways: by helping ensure the timely performance of the task, and by improving the image, and competitive position, of the organization.

Example one. A major New York defense contractor often served as subcontractor on aircraft manufacturing projects. The firm's specialty was supplying essential parts for electrical systems. Management searched for a way to keep the prime contractors (the firm's clients) informed of progress without tying up the firm's own senior management in endless hand-holding sessions. At the same time, the chief executive officer was concerned that the firm's recent doubling in size was leading to schedule slippages that could ultimately alienate key clients.

One of the project managers proposed an EIS, and the chief executiveembraced the idea. Within six months, they had an operating EIS that produced 2,000 project management charts per week. Some of the charts showed project status in Gantt format. Others showed resource utilization. All were clear, looked professional, and communicated with top management.

At first, not everyone was enthusiastic about the EIS. One seasoned project manager feared that the system would give top management "a little knowledge—just enough to make them dangerous." Three months after the EIS was in place, the same individual had been converted. Management now knew more about what was going on, but that worked to the project manager's advantage. "He sometimes notices things I've missed," said the manager, "and he helps me get the extra resources I need when I need them. He knows my needs are real."

In addition, the firm sends some of the project management charts to its clients—the prime contractors. A number of those clients expressed their appreciation in writing for the ease with which they could extract useful information from the EIS charts.

An even larger aerospace firm used similar project management tools. The executive in charge of project management summed up the firm's experience. "The EIS is our most important sales tool. The guys we work for at Defense said our reporting set a new standard and that they now want similar reports from all of their contractors. I am certain that our EIS played a key role in two large procurements we won this past year."

Example two. A New Jersey pharmaceutical company, referred to earlier in this book, spent hundreds of millions of dollars to identify and test new drugs. On average, though, the firm found only one successful drug out of every 10,000 compounds it discovered. Despite these odds, their researchers often became emotionally attached to their most recent discoveries and wanted to continue exploring certain drugs after countless deadends. The search for knowledge is a scientist's prime motivation.

Senior management wanted to be certain that enough resources were being applied to the most important compounds. To make wise decisions, management needed to know what each researcher was investigating, the status of the research, and what effects had been identified for the compounds under examination. The executives also needed to know how much money had already been spent on the compound, and how much more money was needed to get them to the next decision point. None of this information was available. Instead, senior executives relied on anecdotal status reports and estimates from the researchers themselves.

The company implemented a project management EIS focused on its pharmaceutical research. One component combined labor costs, external expenses (clinical trials at universities, for example), project status reports, and project cost estimates. Questions that would have taken hours or days to answer could now be answered in seconds.

This gave senior management unprecedented understanding of, and control over, research resources. It is too early to tell what effect the improved information has had on the quantity of successful new drugs. The EIS has been operational for two years, while the normal gestation period for a new drug is a decade. There has already been one major benefit, however. As the vice president in charge of research laboratories puts it, "The researchers are now more honest about what they are working on. They had developed the bad habit of surreptitiously spending more time on projects that I wanted cancelled. I suspected that they were skimping on projects I felt were most promising. With the new EIS they understand that I will know what they are doing. We can now focus our resources where I believe they will do the most good for the future of this company."

Provide Consistent Information

Most large organizations can benefit from a major EIS business objective: providing consistent management information in one place, at one time. Management meetings too often become a debate over "whose data?" Just providing management with a common set of information would make an EIS worth the investment for thousands of organizations.

Example one. A major New England bank holding company had engaged in an acquisition spree. To catch its breath and assess the situation, the management committee gathered at the bank's Boston headquarters. In attendance were the heads of each operating group, their controllers, and the chief financial officer for the holding company.

The president of the holding company chaired the meeting. He was angry. "You just spent 40 minutes fighting about whose data are right," he fumed. "We spend millions on computers. Can't you get your act together and come up with one set of numbers?" Then, glaring at the chief financial officer, he stated, "I want this problem fixed, and I want it fixed now!"

How bank executives responded illustrates a key point. In EIS development, a single common data base is not enough. You also need a *common set of views* of the data base.

Within seven months after the president issued his marching

orders, the CFO had an operational EIS, which has become the primary source of most management information. The system also met another objective by introducing a corporate standard that provided more than half of the answers that individual systems had been providing. This freed up many of the forty people who had been devoted to writing management-information extraction programs in FOCUS, IFPS, and Lotus 1-2-3 for their respective executives.

Within two years, the EIS performed the rest of the functions demanded by the individual executives. As for the time freed up by the new EIS, those staff members are now producing *useful* analyses of *accurate* information rather than writing undocumented, ad hoc computer applications.

Critical Success Factors

Executives envision a firm's future and make employees work toward that vision. Management, at its best, is a self-fulfilling prophecy. In other words, the executive defines a goal, gets others to work toward it, and ensures its achievement through monitoring, resource management, leading, and cajoling.

To a great extent, it is this simple truth that is at the center of the critical success factors debate. A group of consultants, including Gary Gulden of Index Systems in Cambridge and John Rockart at MIT's Center for Information Systems Research, champions the search for critical success factors.

Under this paradigm, when a company or division identifies its critical success factors, it has discovered the elements of the business that really matter. An example of a critical factor in the pharmaceutical industry would be timely discovery of new marketable drugs. For the automobile industry, a critical factor would be lowering manufacturing costs.

Critical success factors are not limited to corporate entities. Departments within corporations also may define factors critical to the success of their individual missions. For example, two of the critical success factors for data processing operations are ensuring that information systems initiatives are synchronized with overall business objectives, and improving top management's appreciation for data processing activities.

For a fee, management consultants will work with top executives to determine critical success factors for the industry, the company, and/or the department. It is tempting to believe that the process will provide great benefits. Once an organization knows where it should pay attention, it can use its resources more effectively. Further, an executive information system should be far easier to create in an organization that knows its critical success factors. Simply select a factor, aim the EIS at the data that measures how well the factor is being accomplished, and voila! Unfortunately, things often don't work that way.

Trivial Pursuits?

In the hands of inexperienced management consultants, the quest for critical success factors may not be worth the cost. Typically, a consulting firm offers to identify the factors critical to the client's success, for a fee. The client agrees to pay approximately $250,000 and invest six months of top management time working with the consultants.

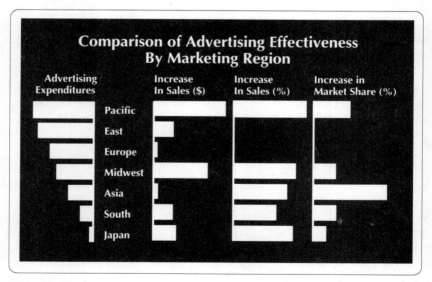

The relationship between advertising expenditures and sales in various markets is a typical success factor. The EIS display above effectively combines several bar charts. If there were a linear relationship between advertising expenditures and sales, then all of four charts would be shaped like the inverted pyramid of the chart at the left.

Then the fog rolls in. The consulting firm assigns a team with limited senior management experience and little background in the client's industry. The client is besieged by a team of bright self-starters whose interviews can absorb hundreds of hours.

There is a hidden hazard in this type of investigation. Because the youthful consultants do not immediately command respect, they may be relegated to the care of one of the client firm's mid-level executives. If senior managers distance themselves from the exercise, the project may become a search for consensus at the middle-management level. The final project report may accurately identify the critical success factors, but without top management involvement the factors will probably not gain the attention they deserve.

Because of these and other problems, some of the very people who helped formulate the concept of critical success factors now argue that the concept has lost its edge—becoming trivialized and routinized.

How could critical success factors have been a good idea a decade ago and be a bad idea today? The value of the idea itself has not changed. However, without having exceptionally talented Renaissance women and men conduct the interviews and build consensus, the idea may not live up to expectations. To weigh a consulting firm's potential usefulness, review their experience with other firms in your industry. If they are true experts in the industry's business problems, objectives, and opportunities their knowledge will be readily apparent.

If the organization has identified its critical success factors, they certainly should be used as a starting point for discussions with EIS-sponsoring executives. However, the executive must be *personally* committed to the success factors in order to be excited about a system that monitors those factors. The executive information system needs to satisfy the executive sponsor, not an outside consultant or mid-level manager.

An extension of the idea of critical success factors is gaining proponents among both academics and EIS consultants. These are critical failure factors—indicators which can tell whether a project or organization is fatally flawed and likely to go under. The most common example is old data in an EIS. If an EIS primarily delivers data that is older than data contained in other reports, the system is likely to fail. Some agree that the opposite—providing very current information—is a critical success factor.

While they may be two sides of the same coin, both success and failure factors are worthwhile concepts for finding indicators to monitor in an EIS. For example, if the senior executive says that the company can no longer afford to be unresponsive to clients, he has defined a critical failure factor. Indicators to monitor that factor could be delay times or number of complaints. Reducing such negative indicators could be a useful outcome of an executive information system.

Some EIS Anchors

There are a number of fringe benefits that can be implemented along with an EIS. While none of these, by itself, would justify EIS development, taken together they offer useful services which can help to garner support for, and institutionalize, the EIS. They can serve to anchor your EIS flagship through the storms to come.

Among the most useful EIS anchors is electronic mail. Other common anchors are executive schedule or calendar packages. Electronic mail, once it catches on, becomes something executives cannot live without. In firms with widely scattered departments, or peripatetic executives, electronic mail can anchor the entire EIS in place.

Executive scheduling packages, on the other hand, are the province of the executive secretaries. They will either love or hate the packages, depending upon whether their bosses stick to, or break, their schedules.

Another EIS fringe benefit to consider is access to external data bases via timesharing with commercial services. What services are chosen, and how much they are worth to the organization, are decisions for the sponsoring executive.

In addition to those already mentioned, other easily implemented EIS accessories include: meeting schedulers, customer and executive profiles, and a telephone directory. Home office meeting schedulers are included in some EIS systems. This feature gives regional executives access to the meeting schedules of the executives at the home office. This allows them to learn about meetings they may want to attend. Such a capability is especially useful in government organizations.

Customer profiles allow the executive to call up, in an instant, a profile of an important client. Short customer profiles can be valuable to any executive who speaks with an important client. Profiles include any level of detail that is justified by your organization's mode of dealing with clients. At a minimum, the customer profile should include what the client likes and dislikes, special problems, and volume and character of their business. Any recent customer complaints should be noted, along with how the complaint was resolved. Customer profiles can also contain personal information (birthdays, children's names, etc.). Such information is easily abused and is more trouble than it's worth.

Profiles of the firm's executives are especially useful in large companies and to new executives. EIS-based executive profiles provide a valuable lubricant for internal relations. Background information on each other, and on lower-level managers, will help executives to understand each other better.

A telephone directory is only useful if it is instantly available and up-to-date. Under those conditions, however, it can be a widely-used EIS tool, second only to electronic mail in large, multi-site organizations.

Electronic Mail

In its simplest form, an electronic mail system substitutes electrons for printed letters and computer displays for paper. The most important prerequisite for a useful electronic mail system is that the key participants be comfortable with, and have access to, computer terminals or personal computers connected to the mail system. All of the "key" people with whom your sponsoring executive needs to interact must be accessible via the electronic mail network. Work with your executive sponsor to identify the people who must be on the system. After this is done, you need to motivate these people sufficiently to use an electronic mail system once it is in place. This can require more investment of time and resources than can be afforded early in EIS development.

When it comes to motivation, the user is a tough nut to crack. But, if the executives know they'll be left in the dust if they don't read their electronic-mail, motivation is no problem. Hence, the best way to motivate users is for the senior executive to say, "I am going to use the electronic mail system to send you messages. Please use the system to respond." As long as the target executives have a terminal or properly equipped personal computer, they or their secretaries will use the electronic mail system. Another way to motivate key users is to give them portable terminals with which to access the system from home or while traveling.

Before implementing any electronic mail system, make certain it is user friendly. Very user friendly. A person wirth a technical background, or even someone who has no trouble setting up and using a VCR, is the wrong person to determine whether or not the system is user-friendly. Have a computer-naive friend test drive the system first.

An electronic mail system should allow access via remote (dial-up) terminal, simple English user controls, automatic multi-party message distribution, and feedback to the sender indicating who has received the message. In addition, the system must offer solid security based upon keywords known only to, and easily changeable by, the individual users. Finally, the system should have a back-up system that allows the recovery of a message which has been accidentally erased.

Look for an electronic mail system with a reliable central repository and communication system. Within a single office, electronic mail can be run on a local area network that connects personal computers. Be certain, however, to allow for dial-up access for executives on the move. Insular departments within large organizations often find that a local-area-network-based system is sufficient.

For most organizations, a far larger network of potential users will need access. In those cases, the electronic mail system will be supported by a host computer. Electronic mail requires only a small portion of a computer system, and would normally be installed on the host computer you already have.

Access to External Data

There are hundreds of major databases available through the dozen or so popular commercial timesharing services. These range from ever-popular stock market quotes to obscure government air-quality models. Using these systems, your executives can do everything from scheduling airline flights, to booking hotels and locating the nearest restaurant that serves sashimi, or getting price and performance information on the competition.

Access to external databases can garner considerable support for your EIS. Approach them with caution. Commercial database systems have two major drawbacks. First, they cost money whose expenditure will have to be justified at some point. Second, they offer a plethora of services, many of which are of marginal use to the busy executive.

Be a skeptic when it comes to selecting external data services. Make them sell themselves on their own merits, and be certain they are bottom-line justified in the eyes of your sponsoring executive. Limit the service(s) you choose to those which are of clear *practical* utility. Take care not to let external data services become toys which clutter your EIS and distract executives from the business at hand.

Our experience shows that EIS vendors and buyers put a far greater value on external data bases than they are worth. Today's executive already has too much data. Or, better put, too much *extraneous* data. Adding an extensive, nonselective library of external sources, especially general data services, just compounds the problem. In the immortal words of Alexander Pope, "Words are like leaves, and where they abound/ Much fruit of truth beneath is seldom found." Or, as Marshall McLuhan succinctly paraphrased, "Less is more."

Most executives, when asked about external data sources, refer only to stock market quotations. Stock market information is easy to find and easy to use. Unfortunately, except to the market itself, stock prices are seldom a crucial business resource. When asked to pay part of the cost of an on-line service, one executive observed, "If I knew we were spending that much on it, I would never have used it. I can get the same stuff from the *Wall Street Journal.*"

To make external data a useful part of an EIS requires two things: the data must be pre-screened to ensure that it is of *direct* use to the executives. And, the selected data must be reformatted to fit the executives. This requires a screening and formatting program, and/or person, between the external data source and your executive clientele.

At Phillips Petroleum, the firm's customary report and graph formats are applied to external data as well. Each display is refreshed with new data at appropriate intervals. Commodity prices, for example, are refreshed every two hours. To get the data, the executive simply gains access to the firm's EIS. Commodity price charts do not require extra keystrokes, special codes or requests. There is no wait for the data.

The EIS allows top executives at Phillips to combine their decades of experience with nearly instantaneous monitoring of international price trends. The system forges a link between the data and the people who trade petroleum products. Some credit the firm's EIS with many millions of dollars in extra profits.

Similarly, the General Motors EIS monitors international currency data. The system screens and reformats the data and updates the information several times each hour.

External data services also can provide news highlights, the high-technology equivalent of a news clipping service. Through the EIS, executives have access to up-to-date information on news items that may affect the organization. These systems can be especially valuable in widely distributed organizations, such as sales-oriented companies, that depend heavily on their field managers and need to keep them well informed.

Again, news services are most effective when the EIS includes a person to screen the stories, highlighting the most urgent and making certain that all are relevant to corporate interests. Relying on a computer program which scans text just won't do. Too many irrelevant articles will get through and waste executive time. An automobile supplier, for example, who inquires about "Ford" would be interested in anything to do with Ford Motor Company. The supplier could care less, however, about former President Jerry, Frances Coppola, or Tennessee Ernie. Solving such problems automatically awaits true artificial intelligence capabilities.

Other, even more intriguing, EIS data sources include the U.S. Congress's system. That system provides superb issue briefs to members of Congress and their staffs. Another valuable source is the *New York Times* data bank which contains the full text of articles from the *Times* and other periodicals. The system includes data that goes back a decade or more, and is especially useful in tracking the background of a firm or reviewing the recent experiences of an individual with whom the executive may be meeting.

Scheduling

One of the simplest accessories to an executive information system is an activity scheduling system. Like electronic mail, these systems work best when all of the key executives participate.

Scheduling systems maintain updated calendars for the firm's key people. They produce daily schedules for each executive and can be invaluable in coordinating meetings which are to include several very busy people. Any scheduling system can be useful, but executive secretaries often find them lacking because of a few features that common programs do not offer. Experienced executive secretaries understand that executives have various ways of scheduling a meeting: sometimes they promise to attend but actually send a substitute (the tag-team approach), or they attend for five minutes and leave (the cameo), or they actually attend the entire meeting (the real thing). Scheduling packages ignore these subtleties. To make them explicit would be rude to the folks who thought they were on the executive's schedule. In other words, even with the world's best EIS scheduler, the experienced executive secretaries will need to maintain a private calendar. This will either be in addition to, or in lieu of, the on-line calendar.

Time Is the Essence

There are two cardinal rules to ensure adequate involvement on the part of the executive sponsor. The first is to avoid wasting the sponsor's time. The second is to adapt to the executive's style of management. Each time an EIS component is demonstrated to the executive, it must work. Each meeting should end with the executive clearly briefed on what the next step should be, how long it will take, and how much it will cost. The executive may change the marching orders, but at least the change will be based upon good information.

Close interaction with the executive requires flexibility on the part of the EIS developer. Meeting times will change unexpectedly. The length of meetings will vary. The EIS director must be able to adjust to fit the executive's schedule. It is a good idea for the EIS director always to prepare two briefings, one for a full-length meeting, and the other for use if the time available is less than half the amount scheduled.

It is essential to maintain a deep respect for the *executive's* schedule. If an executive has nothing scheduled, it should be assumed that it's because *he or she has scheduled to do nothing.* Executive time is theirs to do with as they see fit.

As we said earlier, an EIS isn't going to work if it doesn't reflect the needs of the sponsor. It can't reflect those needs if the EIS developer doesn't know what they are. One of the most important skills required of the EIS developer is the ability to *listen carefully* to what the executive wants. The time spent demonstrating the EIS should be minimized, and the time spend eliciting executive feedback, advice, and suggestions should be maximized. The EIS will belong to that executive to the extent that he or she has had a central role in its design and tailoring.

Another important skill for an EIS developer is to *be interesting*. Executives need to know what is going on, especially at other companies. Good, accurate, relevant information about what others are doing with information technology will be welcome to most executives. The more 'inside' the information is, the better. (No unsubstantiated rumors, please.)

To maintain executive interest, it is essential that the EIS development process *avoid tedious detail*. When someone asks what time it is, they don't want a lecture on the internal workings of a wristwatch. When an executive asks a "how" question, the answer is best if presented in fifteen words or less. More detail should be offered only on request. An EIS should convey only what's important. So should an EIS developer.

6 Hardware Considerations: This Ain't No Candy Store

For an eye-opening experience, attend an EIS vendor demonstration. Listening to the presentations and looking at the displays offer a glimpse of the most advanced EIS systems in existence. Like a kid in a candy store, you'll want it all.

This ain't no candy store. The hardware configuration chosen to run an EIS can account for 80 percent or more of the initial system cost. On the other hand, use existing systems and hardware can be free. Hardware decisions will determine the ultimate cost of the EIS. Make them with care.

Which hardware platforms are best for EIS? That depends on existing systems, budget, and the necessary EIS capabilities. Executive information systems can use personal computers, local area networks, minicomputers, or a centralized mainframe for data manipulation and storage. Modes of access to an EIS range from simple terminals or low-cost personal computers, to powerful microcomputers, or state-of-the-art graphics workstations. Some executive information systems support an almost unlimited array of access modes.

Choice of hardware also determines the nature of the EIS and its future flexibility. Hardware influences the system's responsiveness, whether it offers consistent information to multiple users, and the effectiveness of its visual output. In the final analysis, however, the choice of hardware does not determine the success or failure of the resultant EIS. Hardware choices matter, but they are not the be-all and end-all of the EIS world.

Hardware Choices

Selecting EIS equipment involves three hardware selections: the executive workstation, the EIS host computer to store and manipulate the information, and the display hardware for EIS presentations at meetings and briefings.

There are so many factors that influence the hardware decision that it is impossible to offer a straightforward cookbook or checklist selection guide. In this chapter we discuss the key strengths and weaknesses of the major hardware alternatives.

But first, a chicken-or-egg question: Which should be selected first, the EIS software or the hardware to run it? Some EIS developers advise selecting software first and then getting hardware to run it. In our experience, however, an EIS works better the other way around. The instant you get the go-ahead to develop your EIS, you will be in a big hurry. Buying and installing new host computers and local area networks are more time-consuming than buying software. Waiting for hardware can cause delays.

The Devil You Know

Experienced EIS directors concur: when it comes to hardware, and especially the EIS host computer, the best choice is what already exists on-site. Working within the system by using existing hardware has several major benefits, in addition to lowering costs. First, it speeds implementation of the first EIS application. With existing hardware, there is no need to wait for new hardware. The faster first applications are implemented, the easier it is to maintain momentum and credibility with top management. A partial exception to this rule is the executive workstation. If executives do not yet have workstations, then give them equipment with the speed and control needed to do the job well.

Another benefit of using existing equipment is that it reduces the visibility of the EIS project. Little or no new equipment means business as usual. Less visibility allows more flexibility to correct mistakes in private, sheltered from the glare of peer group ridicule. The less EIS hardware costs, the fewer people will see it as taking a bite out of their piece of the capital pie.

Using existing host computers also avoids offending the people who acquired the hardware in the first place. Purchasing a separate minicomputer or mainframe for the EIS runs the risk of alienating the data processing staff—the very people whose cooperation may be essential to the EIS's success.

Working within the existing hardware environment will simplify access to data. To be effective, an EIS must link the executive to key *sources* of data. Introducing new, non-standard equipment between the executive and the data source is sometimes unavoidable, such as when a mainframe data source is overloaded and cannot provide essential consolidation and transformation functions. However, new hardware can cause political headaches.

Extensive new hardware begets a new data processing staff. New staff competes with existing staff. In a short time competition can displace cooperation.

The existing host computer is appropriate for EIS if it has enough capacity to update the executive information repository. You can claim this capacity whenever appropriate, even on the graveyard (midnight-to-8:00 a.m.) shift. Once the data is updated, the new displays can be sent to the personal computers and executive terminals via your standard network. Your existing computer must, of course, have sufficient power to support centralized EIS software to create the data, analysis, and graphics.

Starting with existing hardware will save money, speed start-up, lower risk, and avoid alienating key staff. Take heart, once a successful system is built, resources for new hardware will become available. On the other hand, if the firm is still relying on punched cards and Teletype machines, don't wait long before pointing out the need for new hardware. In such an extreme case, advent of an EIS can provide an opening for the data center staff to finally get some new equipment. They'll love it.

Dueling Staffs

If the EIS needs a new computer or local area network, it will also need a staff to program and manage the system. There are a few steps that will help avoid the problems of a collision between the EIS staff and the existing data center staff.

Start by relying on the existing data processing staff for advice. Obtain their consent in selecting hardware. Work with current data processing personnel to clearly define inter-computer data communications requirements before purchase of the new system. Include specifications in the request for proposals for the new system which will make the new hardware vendor responsible for ensuring that information can be transferred, quickly and easily, between the existing and the new computers.

While politics and personalities may interfere, the best organizational approach to an EIS is, like the hardware approach, to use the existing resources. Wherever possible, have a member of the existing data processing structure manage the new computer equipment. This not only cements relationships with the existing staff, but also increases the probability that resources needed will be readily available during the crunches to come.

Multiple platforms

Using existing hardware, what happens where the firm already owns multiple hardware platforms? Which should be chosen for the EIS?

The hardware environments that are equally successful as EIS platforms are either terminals or personal computers connected to a responsive EIS host computer (one that responds to a request within a second or two), or personal computers connected to a local area network. In the latter case, one of the personal computers serves as host, and can operate alone or be further connected to a responsive or unresponsive (overloaded) larger host computer. Any of these environments can serve an EIS. The choice depends on factors (such as existing hardware) unique to each organization.

Defining the host computer hardware environment at the start limits software choices. The EIS software will need to work on the chosen hardware. This will save the time that might otherwise be wasted investigating software that won't work with the chosen hardware. The opposite is seldom true. Few EIS organizations are so flush with resources, especially during the early stages of development, that they can select software and then purchase the optimal EIS host hardware.

If the organization already has one or more local area networks, there is an additional option. Using a local area network can avoid the mainframe/minicomputer host route entirely. A powerful microcomputer with a large-capacity disk as the EIS repository, or file server, can be the perfect host for an executive information system. This configuration works if all the executives who will use the EIS are on the same local area network. If executive users are on many different local area networks, or on none at all, then the local area network route is not much better than stand-alone personal computers. We're not big on stand-alone systems. They impose too many limits for our concept of an effective executive information system.

Personal-Computer Isolation

There are six basic hardware configurations for on-line executive information systems: mainframe or minicomputer with terminals; mainframe or minicomputer with personal computers; mainframe or minicomputer with a local area network serving personal computers; mainframe computer *and* a minicomputer *and* personal computers; local area network serving personal computers; and stand-alone personal computers.

All but one of these configurations serves EIS users well. The one that doesn't, stand-alone personal computers, can sometimes be a way station on the road to a better choice. EIS systems work by helping executives propel their organizations toward correcting problems or meeting new, growth-oriented objectives. If the executive is the only person who sees the displays, then the others who need to be influenced by the executive's priorities do not have access to that data.

In such cases, the executive information system fails to meet its potential. The moment you live with an EIS used by a multitude of executives, the weakness of an EIS on stand-alone personal computers is apparent.

Stand-alone personal computers are least effective when an EIS serves many executives, far-flung locations, or numerous organizations. Personal computers that are not connected with those of other EIS users create updating problems for the EIS. These problems can readily undermine executive faith in the system. Then, to keep data up-to-date, the EIS database must be refreshed whenever there is a change in the data. Communications between personal computers that are not connected to a network is uncertain at best, and nonexistent at worst. Secretaries can be asked to retrieve floppy disks from one computer and load them to another, but not on an hourly or even daily basis. Besides, what if they make a mistake, or if the personal computer to which they want to add new data is not configured correctly to receive the update. The number of ways that a stand-alone EIS system can fail is too large for comfort.

Centralization vs Distribution

The three most popular EIS hardware configuration choices are personal computers directly linked to a host computer, personal computers connected to a local network served by the host, or personal computers linked to a small host computer that is further linked to a larger one. Each of these three configurations brings with it a series of decisions about how much data to distribute to the executive's personal computer, how much to leave on the host computer, and where to do the computing to format reports and graphs for display on the executive's workstation.

These decisions lie along a sliding scale. At one end of the scale is the option to download all information from the host to the personal computer and store it there, ready for instant retrieval. At the other end of the scale, all of the data is stored on the central host which responds to requests from the executive's personal computer. Alternatively, any point along the scale can be selected and the personal computer sent a portion of the information with the rest stored on the host.

The controversy over where to house EIS data is exacerbated by competition between the two oldest vendors of EIS software. Not surprisingly, one of these vendors offers primarily centralized approaches and the other adheres to distributed systems. This competition between vendors is one of the main reasons that so much is written, and still more is said, about the benefits of either centralization or decentralization. We feel that you can have the best of both worlds.

Proponents of the centralized approach argue that systems in which all the data is centrally stored and sent to personal computers only when requested instill confidence and save money. Centralization instills confidence by ensuring that everyone has access to exactly the same data at the same time. After all, there is only one source. Each EIS user is looking at an instantaneous snapshot of that data at the moment of inquiry. According to this line of reasoning, the EIS director's job and anxiety are eased because there's only one database to worry about.

Centralizers also argue that their approach saves resources. Host computer resources and downloading time are reduced because nothing is sent to the personal computer unless it is requested, and only what is requested is sent. EIS users typically ask for only a small fraction of all possible displays. If an EIS user only wants to see one out of twenty displays, then a centralized system doesn't waste resources sending the other nineteen or storing them remotely. With centralized data, less disk capacity is needed on the personal computers.

These arguments are cogent and persuasive. So why download the EIS database to the personal computers just to leave it waiting, like Cinderella, for the prince to come? One reason. Speed.

A slow EIS is an oxymoron. (An oxymoron is a large, slow, very stupid beast. Technical name: Bureaucraticus Rex.) Executives want an EIS to get fast answers. If the system requires them to take the time to sign onto the host computer and wait twenty or thirty seconds to retrieve each EIS display, forget it.

How fast is fast enough when it comes to delivering EIS information to your users? Take the executive's point of view. They look upon the EIS as a source of information and advice, sort of like an executive assistant. If the EIS were a human assistant, how long would the executive wait for an answer to a simple question before concluding that the assistant was just plain stupid? Not long.

As a rule of thumb, we find that centralizing the EIS data on the host machine works only if the executive can get EIS-complete displays delivered in approximately five seconds. If your host system cannot consistently deliver the goods quickly, play it safe. Take the distributed path and download the EIS information to the executive's personal computer. Or download to a local a local area network for quick response to executive requests.

Waiting for information from an EIS is a little like being put on hold on the telephone. If the person on the other end and the message to be conveyed are important enough, most people will tolerate a considerable wait. Likewise, executives will wait for information only if the information is very important and they have no choice but to wait. For the EIS to produce a display, a two-second wait is fine. Six to ten seconds pushes the limit of most executives' patience.

If the host computer seems too slow for an EIS, there are a few tricks of the trade that can speed things up. For example, maintain the EIS data on the host computer in pre-formatted displays and reports. These can be computed when host computer time is cheap and available (at night, for example). Then, a small program can be used to deliver the data. This technique will reduce computer resource requirements and improve performance.

Other host computer stimulants include increasing the capacity of communications lines and reducing the demand for that capacity. If all else fails, one can increase the priority that the host computer assigns to executive EIS requests. This latter option has some serious drawbacks. For example, what happens to the EIS when, not if, a higher-priority job comes along?

If everything has been tried and the host computer is still asleep at the switch, don't despair. The system can still realize some of the benefits of centralized information storage through what we call *cascading information delivery*. Every EIS contains a few displays with information in great demand. Many other displays, while necessary, are seldom requested. The EIS can download the popular displays to each personal computer, and retain rarely requested data in the host system. At first, it will be necessary to guess which displays will be in greatest demand, and which can be assigned second-class status. As usage increases, user demand will require adjustment of the distribution of displays. A little experimentation, along with a good record-keeping system showing how frequently each display is accessed by each executive, will provide the information needed to fine-tune the system.

Terminal Executives

For those who have chosen the centralized approach to an executive information system, it is still necessary to decide what to put on the executives' desks—terminals or personal computers. Many successful EIS systems use terminals instead of personal computers as their EIS executive workstations. Implementing an organization-wide electronic mail system is a snap with a terminal-based EIS and centralized database. Terminals linked to an existing host computer also take full advantage of a fringe benefit of a centralized system—they use existing, tested, and proven security systems.

As mentioned earlier, the major objections to centralized EIS include complaints that mainframes take too long to send complex graphic images to the terminal, that mainframes are unreliable and unresponsive, and that executives object to the annoying task of logging on. We also discussed benchmarks for the responsiveness of centralized EIS systems. The problem of requiring executives to sign on can be circumvented simply by leaving the executive's terminal on, an inexpensive solution if the network does not use external communications resources.

Ralph Kennickell, Jr., who used an EIS to revitalize the Government Printing Office, chose terminals instead of personal computers. "We already had terminals in place," he explains. "Why should I spend the money and waste the time waiting for personal computers? Besides, give some people a personal computer, and they'll spend all day playing games. We have a business to run, and don't need any added distractions."

Kennickell's pragmatism is convincing. Why spend the money on personal computers unless they will be used for work that needs to be done? Another reason for using terminals as EIS workstations is that the alternative, personal computers, are too easy for the user to scramble. Terminals are virtually bulletproof.

However, if saddled with an overloaded, unreliable mainframe with slow communication to its terminals, trying to add the EIS could be the straw that breaks the system's back. This is the main reason why most organizations choose personal computers to deliver their executive information.

The Executive Personal Computer

As executives become more computer-literate, they tend to want more independent computing power at their fingertips. In fact, sophisticated workstations, with the kind of graphics and data manipulation powers that were formerly reserved for central host computers, are the fastest-growing segment of the computer market.

As personal computers and workstations spread through organizations, more EIS projects are relying upon them as data conduits. Where personal computers are already in place, it makes very little sense to add EIS terminals to the executives' crowded desks.

If you decide to use personal computers with your mainframe or mini, there remain two important decisions: What type of personal computer to use and whether the personal computer will be dumb or smart. A dumb personal computer is one which merely serves as a terminal. A smart personal computer, on the other hand, can function as a powerful workstation. Or, you can have both. The personal computer can be either terminal or independent processor, at the executive's whim.

In a sense, this is a software question. But it is a decision which should be made before investigating alternative software packages. How EIS personal computers function defines the environment in which the executive will work. If the personal computer is used as a graphics terminal, it offers all the benefits of a mainframe-with-terminal EIS configuration, and exactly the same detriments. This approach only makes sense if the central mainframe or mini is powerful enough, has adequate unused capacity, and has sufficient communications resources.

Which personal computer is selected—IBM AT compatible, PS/2, Macintosh, or other—can be a time-consuming and politically sensitive decision. "Our executives don't want computers at all," complained one EIS director, "but their secretaries all have Macintoshes. The MIS director wants IBM compatibles and drools like one of Pavlov's dogs at the mention of a PS/2. I personally prefer Macintosh, but I'm stuck between a rock and a hard place."

This debate can turn unpleasant if access to the executive information system is determined by who gets the expensive personal computers. In one federal government EIS, for example, we found that many executives in the agency were antagonistic toward the EIS. The budget allowed for only a dozen users, because each EIS workstation cost more than $8,000. When the lucky users were chosen, many more executives and their staffs— especially the staffs—were alienated. They felt that they had been excluded. With continuing tight budgets, the problem has yet to be resolved. In the meantime, the effectiveness of the EIS is compromised by the lack of widespread EIS access.

Regarding workstation hardware, in general, it is also advisable to use hardware that is already in place. If some executives don't have workstation hardware, then it is wise to buy the most advanced compatible systems the EIS can afford. However, refrain from designing a system which requires every executive to install a high-priced workstation in order to use the EIS.

LAN Ho!

Another point on the scale between centralized and distributed data is defined by the local area network (LAN). By linking all EIS personal computers together and to the host system, a local area network can also help solve the problem of an unresponsive mainframe. Used effectively, it can alleviate the need to download EIS data to each and every executive personal computer. However, LAN-based systems currently have some drawbacks. The networks, by themselves, do not provide the extra processing power the EIS may require. They may also lack well-managed security systems; and they offer only limited access to the vast quantities of data available from the mainframe.

A local area network strategy works best in organizations that already have networks in place, want to deliver fixed displays to the executive, and have difficulty using the mainframe as a file server. To the executive personal computer, a file server makes the mainframe or local area network data files look as though they are on a disk connected directly to the personal computer. With a fast, effective file server, many personal computers can share access to the same EIS files. A mainframe or minicomputer can be a useful file server, as well, if it has speed and responsiveness. If not, a personal computer with a lot of storage capacity, connected to a local area network may serve as the best repository for the EIS tables and charts.

The problem with local area networks is not their performance. Generally, their performance is excellent. The problem is that most local area networks are just that—local. Most serve only a few dozen people in a single location or department. If fifty or sixty executives are to use the EIS from different locations, then data will have to be downloaded to as many local area networks as necessary.

Downloading to local area networks is not as risky as downloading to many more personal computers. However, it still creates the possibility of one user seeing today's data while another is looking at yesterday's. If one of the local area networks fails to receive updated information, there is always the chance of different executives seeing and arguing over different versions of the same data with no easy way to discover their problem. In spite of this potential weakness, rapidly advancing technology, including gateways and bridges between LANS, is making local area networks the clear choice among EIS directors for their preferred future information distribution technique.

The Wedding-Cake Approach

More than sixty organizations use a three-tiered wedding cake structure for their executive information systems. The base of the structure is the mainframe. It houses the data and sends extracts to the next layer. The next layer consists of a minicomputer which stores, manages, and analyzes the data. On top, connected to the minicomputer, are the personal computers on executives' desks.

Proponents of this approach argue that it is the only practical solution when a mainframe is entirely unresponsive and the EIS must guarantee every user access to exactly the same data. This isn't necessarily so. In some cases, an unresponsive mainframe can be revived by using the mainframe as a file server or virtual disk. This technique can sometimes avoid the normal delays associated with the timesharing system.

A problem with the three-tiered approach is that larger applications on the minicomputer can require an additional data processing staff, with the associated management challenges. Established information system people may argue that, for the cost of the new minicomputer and the staff to support it, they could have added the capacity to make their original mainframe do the job.

These arguments in no way discredit the wedding-cake approach. It is a viable alternative, but should be weighed carefully against either augmenting the existing mainframe or adding a local area network rather than a separate minicomputer.

Display's the Thing

Thus far, we've concentrated on display systems for use on or near the executive's desk. To realize its full potential, the EIS must be able to produce displays that can be used in executive sessions and board meetings. Such display capabilities require two more hardware systems. One system produces printed or slide copies of the EIS displays. The other projects EIS charts onto screens so that a large audience can view them.

Large-scale displays come in two forms: standard transparencies (slides) and real-time, on-line systems. Most EIS directors start with a preference for the real-time approach because it avoids the extra steps, delays, and errors that can be introduced in the process of making transparencies. But, this may betray a touch of technophilia. Our experience shows that many EIS directors change their minds and switch back to the low-tech, but reliable, slides and transparencies.

Why switch back? Four reasons: Brightness, sharpness, reliability, and cost. Real-time displays cost from $700 to $75,000, with performance directly proportional to price tag. At the entry level is the black-and-white liquid crystal display (LCD) panel. This panel, about the size of a large-format book, is a slave to your terminal or personal computer. It merely copies what is displayed on the terminal. You can place an LCD panel on a standard overhead projector. Whatever you see on the terminal also appears on the LCD panel and, therefore, is projected onto the screen. It is intended to work as though the LCD panel were a black-and-white overhead. Almost.

The images created by LCD panels of this type convey information, but with serious drawbacks. They are not as bright as standard transparencies, and the contrast is not as high. As a result, they are not as easy to read, especially under less-than-ideal circumstances. The terminal or personal computer, and therefore the LCD panel, has far less resolution than the standard overhead transparency produced on a laser printer. Rather crude. Lack of color, lack of brightness, lower contrast, and inferior resolution make these display monitors less than a joy to work with. Not very impressive, either.

Color LCD panels, which are just hitting the market, will solve the color problem, but the brightness and resolution remain mediocre. The price tag for the color panels is higher—$3,000 to $5,000 per unit.

The next step up is the 35mm slide magic box. Costing $7,000 to $12,000 with software, these boxes sit next to your personal computer or terminal. At the push of a button, after a minute or two, they produce sharp, full-color film copies of whatever is displayed on your personal computer screen. The slides can be developed just like other color slides. Another type of slide film develops itself in a few minutes, but sacrifices much of the brightness of the slide.

These magic slide machines are a practical alternative for the organization that wants to produce high-quality color slides on short notice. Consider how much the firm already spends on quick-turn-around slide processing. Also consider the associated delays and panics. Organizations often find that an in-house slide-making capability can pay for itself in a very short time. The quality and attractiveness of some of the slides must be seen to be appreciated. Most impressive.

Between $6,000 and $15,000 will buy a color projector that displays full-color images onto a wall or large screen. These devices suffer from some of the same problems as the LCD panel mentioned earlier. Color projectors have low resolution, mediocre contrast, require darkened rooms, and are often difficult to read. They have one additional problem. Unless mounted in the ceiling, out of harm's way, they're stunningly unreliable.

At about $15,000 per unit, the brightness and contrast of color projectors dramatically improve. Moving up from 500-line personal computer displays to 1,000-line displays, the resolution gets better. The bottom line, however, is that large screen color systems rarely meet the needs of executive briefings.

There are exceptions. Phillips Petroleum and John Hancock Insurance, among others, have designed conference rooms especially to accommodate the large-screen projectors. The units are mounted in the ceiling, and lighting is carefully controlled to keep the screens readable without leaving the audience completely in the dark. In some cases, projectors can be located closer to the screens to improve brightness.

These successful systems are expensive. As a rule of thumb, a large-screen projector works well only when installed in a conference or boardroom specifically designed for such a system. Hence, in addition to the cost of the system itself, you'll need to add considerable resources for renovation and lighting of a new conference room.

There is, of course, a top of the line. At about $75,000 per state-of-the-art system, most of your display problems can be solved. Such systems use advanced technology such as light-valve projectors to sharpen contrast and improve brightness. While such a system is very impressive, so is the price tag. Plus, the technology is so advanced that you're going to have fun finding replacement parts or a technician to adjust the projector a half-hour before a board of directors meeting.

For the rest of us, with boundless imaginations but limited budgets, we can either use overhead transparencies from laser printers, produce 35mm slides, or use large cathode ray tube (CRT) displays. Large CRT's range upward from 35-inch diagonal television screens. While these displays have a few drawbacks—they are limited in screen size and can be a bit intimidating—they are very effective. They are also very, very heavy.

Large CRT's have no better resolution than projectors. They cannot improve on the original display shown on the executive workstation. But they greatly improve brightness and contrast. Cathode ray tube technology is better than projection technology. Furthermore, the resolution problems encountered in large-screen projectors are disguised by the smaller size of the television cathode ray tube. Put simply, the pictures do not look as crude on a large television set as they do on a projection system.

Big cathode ray tube displays are priced at about $8,000. Two of them cost approximately the same amount as a decent projection system. Two or three television sets placed strategically around a conference room create an effective real-time system.

It's a Hard-Copy World

Whatever type of boardroom display is selected, the EIS will need high-quality, fast hard-copy equipment. In the early days of computers and timesharing, many wags were predicting the paperless society. No such thing. Per capita demand for paper products is at an all-time high, and still growing.

Paper is a necessity. Executives need to get the most out of their time. Paper remains the most practical medium for reading while in a taxi or airplane. The quality of an EIS paper system must be good. Executives need to feel comfortable enough to include EIS material in memos without having to apologize for poor-quality printout. In addition, high-quality paper displays are essential if they are used to make EIS transparencies as well.

If the organization already owns a sophisticated, four-color pen plotter, EIS developers may be tempted to use it. Don't. Most plotters are painfully slow and unreliable. They also have trouble with shading and tinting. A plotter's idea of color shading is countless parallel lines which don't really add up to much. To have the entire EIS dependent on a pen plotter for its hard-copy output is like climbing a mountain without a safety line. At best, it's a cliff-hanger.

Instead of plotters, laser printers are the rule for black-and-white printing. Use color thermal printers, ink-jet printers, color-ink bead (Cycolor), or color laser printers for EIS color hard-copy and overhead transparencies. All of the above machines are faster, more effective, and more reliable than color pen plotters. They are more expensive, but an EIS is judged by the quality of its output where it counts most—in the executive's hands.

Visit to the Candy Store

In the enviable situation in which the EIS director is given a blank check to acquire new, or upgrade existing, hardware to create the ideal EIS, congratulations. The system can enjoy the best of both worlds—the benefits of a single data base with centralized architecture, and the speed and responsiveness of a distributed system.

On the host computer, the first step is to ensure that there are sufficient communications channels dedicated to the EIS. This is to avoid any chance of contention between EIS information delivery and other host computer uses. Also, be sure to provide enough memory on the host system so that the EIS software does not have to be swapped back and forth between disk and memory. This may sound like a simple request, but a good EIS software system can require more than ten megabytes of memory—a tidy addition for many host systems.

The next step is to buy the best executive terminals available. For IBM host environments, acquire top-of-the-line PS/2 Model 70 computers with the fastest disks available. PS/2 computers offer direct access to multiple mainframe sessions. This allows users to switch instantaneously between, for example, information display and electronic mail. Keep in mind that many users lower in the organization will not have PS/2 systems. The EIS software must support all popular personal computers.

In Digital or other non-IBM host environments, stick with very fast MS-DOS 80386 computers with VGA graphics capabilities (or better) and very fast disks. If your sponsor has a soft spot for Macintosh systems, never fear. The speedy Macintosh II systems are flexible and colorful enough to meet design needs and keep the sponsor happy at the same time.

For paper output, get a color laser printer that can read Post-Script files and print at least four pages per minute at resolutions of 300 dots-per-inch or better. Such devices are now beginning to become readily available. In their absence, the EIS can substitute a color thermal printer, or two if speed is essential. For routine printing, a fast black-and-white laser printer is a must. Printers should be linked via a network so that each executive can print a document at the press of a button on the workstation.

If the firm's executives give slide shows on the road, get a 35mm color slide accessory. Finally, procure a set of large television-like color displays. Locate them throughout the boardroom and other conference rooms. Buy enough of the units so that everyone in the room can see without getting whiplash.

If you still haven't broken the bank, look into infrared controllers and rosewood cabinets. And, please, give us a call.

Who Gets the Keys?

As EIS plans evolve, one of the topics that will influence the choice of hardware is which people, and how many, will have access to the EIS data. In reviewing the list of people who need access to the EIS, consider that an effective EIS often grows rapidly beyond its original boundaries.

One of America's largest retail store chains established a data acquisition network nearly a decade ago. The network allowed more than 94 percent of its stores to report detailed sales data to headquarters every night. By dawn each morning, the IBM mainframe at the company's headquarters had analyzed all the individual store data and produced reports and graphs that summarized the data and highlighted trends.

The system was developed because top management felt it needed more up-to-date sales information to succeed in the highly competitive retail environment. The entire cost of the EIS, the computers, and the communications network, was fully justified by anticipated improvements in management's ability to respond quickly to emerging trends, coupled with the store managers' more careful attention to detail.

The executive information director responsible for creating the system decided that five people needed access to the system. The presumption was that they were the ones who made the big decisions. Given the EIS data, they could then direct others to act quickly, resolve problems, or seize opportunities.

To everyone's surprise, within four months more than 150 senior- and mid-level executives were active users of the EIS data. The organization learned first hand one of the cardinal rules of EIS: A successful system will always spread throughout the management team. In this sense, an EIS can rapidly assume an important leadership role within an organization.

When senior executives learn to trust the information supplied by an EIS, they begin to act on that information. They call subordinates and ask them to explain or investigate information highlighted by the EIS. Or they direct subordinates to take actions based upon problems or opportunities spotlighted by the system.

For example, one day the chairman of that same retail chain noticed that sales had plummeted in the hardware department of one store in Columbus, Ohio. He immediately called the store manager to find out what was wrong. Apparently, a paint spill kept customers off the aisles in question. Store management was stunned at the chairman's knowledge of their activities. Needless to say, every executive in the corporation in any way responsible for merchandising demanded a key to the EIS.

If subordinates do not have access to the same information available to the executive, their hands are tied. They don't know what their bosses know about their own operations. Almost immediately they ask the boss for access to the system. The boss says, OK. The EIS grows. In fact, if a new EIS does not grow beyond a privileged few, this indicates a potential problem. The EIS is probably not being used effectively.

There is another reason why an executive information system spreads. In an earlier chapter we describe the value of using an EIS to motivate and focus an organization on top management's goals. One of the most difficult jobs of an executive is to focus corporate resources on those areas of highest priority. An EIS can be there when the executive cannot.

Using an EIS to reinforce top management priorities works best when the people who do the work get feedback that shows how well they are doing. In other words, when they have access to the EIS. As several chief executive officers have said, put terminals where the work gets done. If those people know what top management thinks is important, and how well they are doing, they will make progress regardless of management's direct involvement.

Who will need access to the EIS? Consider two functions— initiation and implementation. Who is responsible for initiating action if the information in the EIS highlights a problem or an opportunity? Who will implement that action? Who implements the objectives measured by the EIS indicators?

Once the initiators and the implementers are identified, the question of who in the organization is likely to use a successful EIS is answered. That answer also indicates how much hardware the EIS will need.

7 Human/EIS interaction: Read My Lips, Hal

In the movie *2001* Hal, the computer, suffers from terminal paranoia. Hal begins spying on the humans who litter his environment. When the humans try to hide from Hal's voice recognition systems, Hal learns to read lips. Added to Hal's perfect spoken English, a nicer way to interact with an EIS is hard to imagine. On the other hand, Hal's efforts to exterminate the crew can hardly be called *user friendly*.

Fortunately, most computers are not as homicidal as Hal, and some can process spoken human commands. With the exception of lip reading, today's EIS offers a wide array of tools an executive can use to obtain information from the system.

Access tools include printed reports with easily-understood graphics and color keys, menus on terminal or personal computer screens from which the executive can type requests to the system, and large-scale boardroom presentation systems. In some systems, the executive can point at, or touch, an icon to command the system to display the related information.

Whatever the executive's method of querying the EIS, its presentation format is crucial to the eventual success of an EIS. However, it is unnecessary, and sometimes unwise, to invest a lot of time designing the *initial* presentation screens. Formatting is not a decision that can be front-loaded. Finding out what presentation formats, and what menus, work with each executive is an interactive process. Without real, relevant data, different formats are abstract art. It is far easier for executives to choose from alternative formats when the formats are loaded with the information that they seek. Executives need to see *both* the forest *and* the trees, and will invariably require changes in the initial display. Once the executive has seen some real-life examples, that is the time to fine-tune the format to the user.

Basic Interaction Modes

Executives extract information from an EIS via five mechanisms: paper, keyboard, infrared controller, mouse, and touchscreen. Starting with paper, the EIS ultimately will need to produce clean, attractive paper copies, on demand. With a minimum of fuss, it should create chartbooks for executives who are traveling or who don't want to use the computer directly. To get data from a well-designed paper copy of an EIS, the user need only turn the page. Be sensitive to, and respect, the fact that this is as far as some executives may want to go toward interacting with computers.

Paper is a passive way to deliver executive information. Outside of the fine art of origami, there is little interaction with a paper-based system. This is both a strength and a weakness: a strength because paper reports are both familiar and predictable; a weakness because paper reports are limited in length, format, color, and flexibility.

Some executive information systems use presentation screens which are, in essence, television displays of paper reports. Users interact with the system by turning it on and telling it when to move forward. The EIS presents information pre-programmed for each user. This interaction mode is useful when the executive user wants exactly the same information each hour, day, or week, or where the EIS is designed to provide status information at the worker level of an organization.

The other four interaction mechanisms all control on-screen access to EIS information. Perhaps the most common interaction technique is the menu. A menu presents users with a set of columns listing available displays. Menus can be arranged hierarchically, with subjects of interest to a particular executive grouped in the same menu column. The user can then type into keyboard, press a button on an infrared remote controller, point with a mouse, or touch a spot on the screen to select the number, title, or icon of the display wanted.

When choosing an access method for the executive information system, apply the following criteria: Does it quickly engage the executive? Is it comfortable for long-term, analytical and electronic mail uses? The access method needs to engage a user quickly in order to gain immediate acceptance. Touchscreens and remote infrared controllers require less than thirty seconds to capture the user's attention, and demand no previous experience with computer mice or keyboards. Simple as they seem to the initiated, computer mice can challenge the neophyte. Keyboards are complex, imposing, and not very useful if the goal is to make a quick, positive impression on the executive user.

Long-term comfort is essential if the executive is to continue to use the system. Other access modes—the infrared controller, the mouse, and the keyboard—are important in this context. Believe it or not, people can develop shoulder and wrist problems from being forced to continuously repeat any simple operation such as touching a screen.

Detailed analytical work and electronic mail require that words and numbers be entered into the system. Nothing beats a keyboard for this function. In addition, keyboards can be effective for menu selection, especially on a system that offers single-keystroke speed and ease of use.

In conclusion, touch screen access is most impressive when first presenting the EIS, but the other three methods—infrared controller, mouse, and keyboard—are of enduring importance. To a great extent, each user, when confronted with using the system, will determine the preferred method. As user needs change, the system should respond. Hence, the EIS would do well to support all access methods, including paper.

Alternative Data Formats

The secret may be in the data, but the key to that secret is in the display. One of the most important EIS tasks is design of the data display. The display is what makes the information useful. At some point during the process of tailoring the display format to the executive, the EIS director will invariably feel like a lonely pioneer. Fear not, others have traversed these barren plains before, and survived.

One of the earlier efforts to divine an effective format for executive data was investigated as part of the research for a Department of Defense early warning system. The idea was to head off trouble by using a set of indicators to raise an alarm early enough to act upon it. In 1970, the researchers developed a complex set of mathematical analyses to display trends in military and political indicators around the world. The system stretched the boundaries of mathematical modeling.

Some exceptional minds worked on the indicators, models, and relationships. One of the mathematicians, for example, was awaiting his third graduate degree from MIT. Some exceptionally strange people worked on the project, too. One was a fan of Hitler. The design team recalls, "that guy could have been, probably should have been, institutionalized. He was a genius, all right, but sometimes he would lapse into screaming fits because he thought a locomotive was roaring through his office. No kidding."

Each day the researchers fed the system a range of indicators on every country of concern. The indicators were measures of transport aircraft movements, communications traffic and level of encryption, military readiness status, and so on. The system displayed two dozen indicators for each country. The result was a checkerboard display which was hopelessly complex. The intended audience was top-echelon military executives. They had gained authority not through training in abstract statistical theory, but through skill at their respective crafts: Flying aircraft, running tanks, fighting wars. They wanted the bottom line. They couldn't get it from the convoluted, checkerboard display.

To simplify the display, the designers needed a symbol. They adapted a thermometer to represent a composite of all the indicators. The final result was elegant. As familiar and simple as a home thermometer, the display proved to be both compact and understandable at a glance.

In conclusion, EIS indicators and displays can be a lot of work to develop. However, it's worth investing considerable effort to produce displays and reports which both summarize the data and communicate to an executive-level audience. But what *is* the most effective way to convey executive information? Fortunes have been spent looking for the answer. To observe the state-of-the-art in graphic communications, switch on the evening news, or pick up a copy of *USA Today*, and check the weather page. Don't be deceived by the simplicity of the graphics. Behind the scenes are millions of dollars in equipment and expertise.

A secret of effective communication is to make charts *look* simple without sacrificing essential information. Again, look at *USA Today*'s weather page. One display packs an enormous amount of information in a provocatively attractive package. That's what executive information system displays must achieve.

What makes an effective information package depends entirely on the audience. Some of the early executive information systems directors were curious enough to fund studies of information formats. For example, in 1975, a government security agency sponsored a study to identify the optimum method for presenting their case to Congress. They wanted to know what information format was the best way to show how they were allocating their resources without revealing too much information about exactly what was being done.

The study employed an extensive, and expensive, decision analysis group. It tested six different data formats: graphics, text, three numerical displays, and voice. To determine the effectiveness of the various formats, the study used high-powered teams to represent the target executives.

Their findings were revealing. The researchers found that, regardless of the topic, people have fixed notions of how they expect information to be displayed. Not surprisingly, their preferred data format depended upon their training. They liked the familiar. In addition, people who liked one type of display were very reluctant to consider alternative display formats. It's not just that they were not used to different formats, they were actually hostile to them. Analysis of their responses showed that when they saw a display that was *not* in their favorite format, they assumed someone was trying to hide something. They didn't trust alternative formats.

In our experience, executives are generally more open minded about different information formats. While they may have a certain preference for data for their own use, they have seen enough effective briefings to know what their peers are doing and to know what to expect from an effective communications format. Data for their private use should be in their favorite format. Data for others to use should not only contain the requisite information but should look good. Data for both should both look good and be in the executive's favorite format.

Hey, Good Looking!

One of the more tenacious myths of executive information systems is that they don't need *fancy* graphics. We call this the Sergeant Joe Friday myth, which asserts that executives want "just the facts, ma'am." Nuts.

Of course executives want the facts, but what is fancy graphics to one person is effective communication to another. Fancy graphics, used in the EIS context, are usually sour grapes. The term is often used by an EIS director to describe graphics which cannot be produced using his or her system.

After studying more than a hundred executive information systems, we conclude that the most effective display systems, the ones with the greatest staying power, are those that present boardroom-quality (clear, easy-to-read, well-designed) displays, automatically, on demand. An effective EIS is not just a tool to communicate with a handful of key executives. It is a way of helping an entire operation to focus energy on key goals and to unite to solve problems identified by the executives. This cannot be done in a vacuum. If an organization wants everyone to march in the same direction, it needs to get the message out beyond the confines of a few executive offices. A good EIS is the best way to get the message out.

Most effective executive information systems can create visuals for display on a large television screen, electronic projector, or slides and overheads . In today's highly visual environment, executives are constantly exposed to good graphics. While it may not have been true a decade ago, today's executives know good graphics when they see them. Executives don't like to look shoddy. Unless the EIS can match the best graphics that the graphics designers can produce, it will embarrass, rather than illuminate, the executive sponsors.

Good graphics are good because they communicate. An EIS is nothing if not a communications device. If inferior or ineffective graphics interfere with the EIS's ability to communicate, what's the point? Investment in an EIS without boardroom-quality graphics is like buying a scoop of ice cream without a cup or cone. The substance is there, but without the packaging you won't get the full enjoyment out of it. It won't last as long. And you may end up in a sticky situation.

Your First Screen Test

Now the business objective the EIS will monitor has been selected and the data to monitor progress toward that objective has been identified. The next big step is to select the hardware and software for the prototype. First, however, the presentation formats should be picked. The formats selected to display the data help determine which hardware and software to select.

Depending on the data, audience, and technology, the following are some of the more effective information formats. If some formats seem more effective than others, remember that *all* of them were specifically requested by someone to whom they communicated well. As they say, there's no accounting for taste.

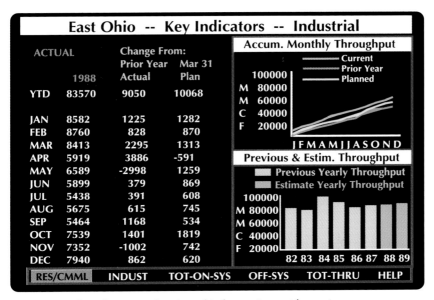

Multi-color charts pack a lot of information. Above is an
Execucom screen using bars, lines, and numbers simultaneously.
Below is an eary stoplight chart from NASA showing two months
status data. Such charts are efficient for meetings and briefings.

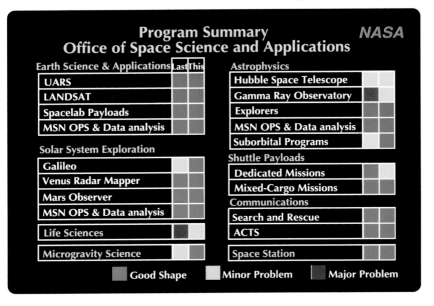

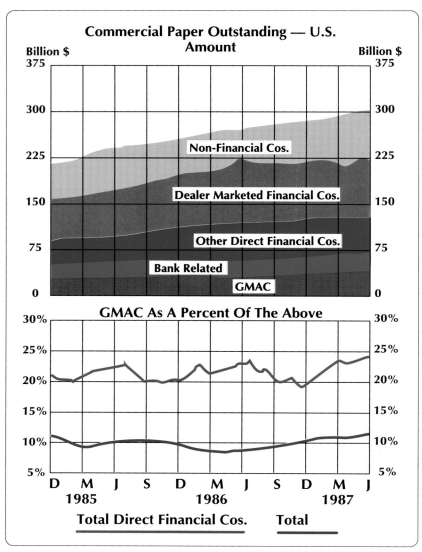

Reproduced above is one page from General Motors' chartbook. GM managers carry the pocket-size books which contain up to 200 pages of sophisticated graphics showing sales, financial and operations trends. As can be seen on page 150, the chartbook is also effective in black-and-white. The 3.5 by 4.5 inch book puts an astounding wealth of up-to-date information in the hands of GM's top 70 managers.

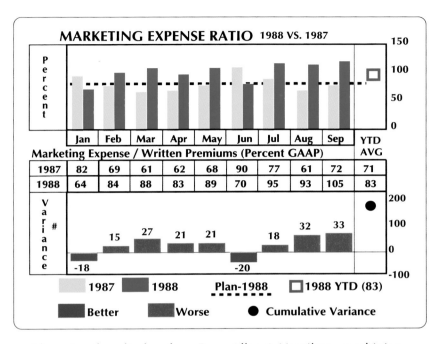

Above is a fine display, from Booz Allen & Hamilton, combining two simple bar charts with a table to satisfy all format preferences. Below, in the format popularized by Consumer Reports, is a table combined with graphic symbols and colors. This type of format is both efficient and comfortable.

Product	Dimensions	Price	Weight	Watt Settings	Fan Speeds	Temp Distrib	Spot Heating	Temp Swing	Noise
Prestomatic	15x21x7	$82	9	2	1				
Edison	13x20x12	55	9.5	2	1				
Markmar	16x11x12	68	7	7	1				
Alvinton	15x22x2	102	11.5	3	1				
Titanson	13x17x12	52	8	2	2				
KWM	12x19x16	50	7.5	2	1				
Model 90	13x19x6	40	6.5	3	1				

Poor
Fair
Good
Very Good
Excellent

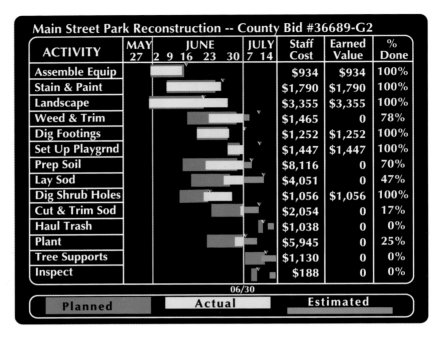

Main Street Park Reconstruction -- County Bid #36689-G2

ACTIVITY	MAY 27	JUNE 2 9 16 23 30	JULY 7 14	Staff Cost	Earned Value	% Done
Assemble Equip				$934	$934	100%
Stain & Paint				$1,790	$1,790	100%
Landscape				$3,355	$3,355	100%
Weed & Trim				$1,465	0	78%
Dig Footings				$1,252	$1,252	100%
Set Up Playgrnd				$1,447	$1,447	100%
Prep Soil				$8,116	0	70%
Lay Sod				$4,051	0	47%
Dig Shrub Holes				$1,056	$1,056	100%
Cut & Trim Sod				$2,054	0	17%
Haul Trash				$1,038	0	0%
Plant				$5,945	0	25%
Tree Supports				$1,130	0	0%
Inspect				$188	0	0%

06/30

| Planned | Actual | Estimated |

For sophisticated project management, not much beats the
Gantt chart. The one above, from CA-Tellaplan, provides more
information on one page than is often conveyed during
a one-hour briefing. Likewise, the group of line charts
illustrated below provides both relative status and historical
trends information at one glance.

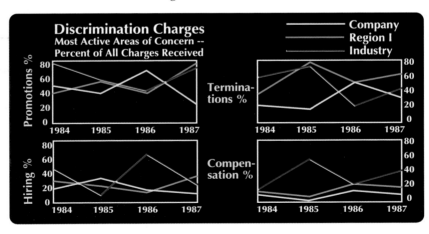

Paper Chase

If every executive stayed in the office all day and had an easy-to-read computer display connected to displays in other executives' offices, then paper-based EIS might not be so all-fired important. But executives are not in their offices all day. They travel on air-planes and in taxis. They visit clients, suppliers, bankers, and competitors. They heed nature's call and visit workers who do not have EIS terminals. And, contrary to common perception, many even go home to be with their families.

Wherever they are, executives may want access to the EIS displays. They also need to send copies of some of those displays to people who are not on the system. In short, they need paper.

The most appreciated paper-based EIS is the pocket-sized chartbook. At General Motors Acceptance Corporation, seventy top executives each get one or more of seven different chartbook covering topics such as internal operations, sales/marketing, and economic indicators. When a GMAC executive is visiting a client and is asked about interest rate trends or revenue patterns, more often than not, the answer is right in his pocket.

Ideal paper-based systems combine detailed tabular information with graphs of that information *on the same page.* This allows the executive user who prefers one format over the other to get that format without requiring the EIS to produce two booklets.

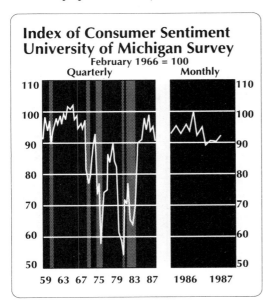

General Motors uses a very effective method for combining multiple line charts. The chart to the left shows two different time periods, using different scales for each period.

In addition, this combination format saves time. The combined presentations are robust: the graphs offer a quick glimpse of patterns and trends, while the tables give the user the precise numbers upon which to act. Quickly

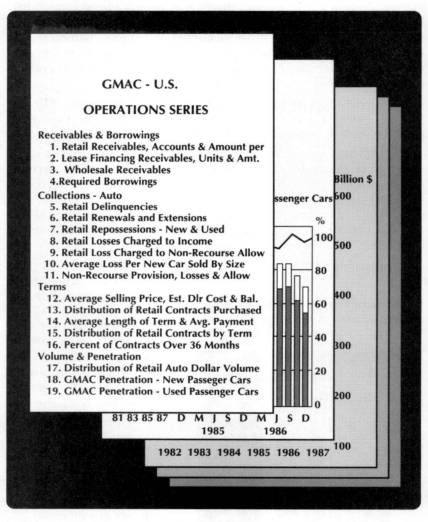

Illustrated above are but a few pages from one of GM"s information-packed chartbooks.

8 EIS Software: The Brain in The Box

No other decision in the EIS development process is as bewildering as the choice of software. The wrong software can hobble efforts, and cause the system to appear unresponsive to executive requirements. To make the situation even more complicated, new EIS software and software systems are sprouting like dandelions after a spring rain.

To help, this volume contains two chapters on EIS software. This chapter deals with software for host mainframe or mid-range computer-based EIS systems. The following chapter covers EIS software available for personal computers. There is considerable overlap and duplication between the two chapters. If the EIS hardware has already been selected, you can skip the chapter which deals with the other configuration.

EIS software packages are sprouting everywhere, and the state of the art is shifting rapidly. Newer packages may entice with more bells and whistles. While it is important to obtain sophisticated EIS software, technology is only a small part of the EIS world. The information itself is the prime focus of an EIS.

The best technology in the world won't save an EIS if it contains the wrong information. On the other hand, almost any technology will work as long as the EIS is delivering the right information, in the right format, to the right person, at the right time. Having reviewed successful EIS systems which deliver data via dozens of different packages, we're convinced that *there are many correct software choices*. We hold to three tenets in making EIS software decisions.

Software Rules

First, pick software that allows the first prototype (using real data) to be operational within less than three months after management approves the project. By approval, we mean acceptance of the idea, not contract sign-off. If it takes longer than three months to reach prototype, experience shows that the executive sponsor's attention and support may cool. It is acceptable to take more time in order to better identify the organization's goals and fine tune the EIS indicators. However, delays caused by balky software are not acceptable.

Second, pick software which is open and able to encompass other packages, rather than software that requires the use of only the tools that a single vendor supplies. As long as the EIS software serves as a gateway to other software packages, and to the reports and graphics produced by the other packages running on the same machine, anything is possible—electronic mail, animation, voicr—anything. Open systems are liberating. They keep the EIS from being held hostage by a single vendor. They also allow for quicker starts and for the continued use of software tools with which staff is already familiar.

Third, pick EIS software which supports all delivery options: on-line, on paper, and presentation. The software should not limit, in any way, the flexibility or quality of the graphics. On-line displays should appear within a few seconds. Invariably the executive served by the EIS will communicate with people who are away from their desks. For them, an effective paper-based EIS systems is essential. Regularly updated pocket chartbooks can travel with the executives and put the information resources of their EIS at their fingertips wherever they roam. Our experience is that EIS systems which emphasize high-quality visuals usually have more staying power and executive acceptance than systems which skimp on visual capabilities.

Large organizations seldom authorize major executive decisions without prior scrutiny by other executives, usually at review meetings. An EIS that provides the information, but doesn't produce the visuals needed to make that information useful during presentations, is only half a system. As mentioned earlier, EIS visuals can be delivered on-line, or as 35mm slides, or overhead projector transparencies. Slides or overheads produced by the EIS should be of excellent quality. They should match those produced by a graphics design shop.

Speed is critical if the system is used for on-line presentations. It must work as fast as a slide projector, or the executive audience will stray. When that happens, the best arguments in the world fall on deaf ears.

Executives are under great pressure when they brief their peers. They need visuals which make just the right argument in just the right way. The most famous words in executive presentation work are "just a few minor changes." If the executive information system is responsible for making the visuals, it had better be able to make all of the changes the executive wants almost immediately. If it can't make those changes, or if the quality of the visuals is less than the quality of other presentations, the EIS is letting the executive down at a crucial moment.

This is such an important point that it will be repeated in the following chapter on using personal computers as the basis for an EIS. Readers who choose to skip this chapter because they plan to use personal computers need to know this point, too. For the rest of our readers, please pardon the redundancy.

Many common choices of EIS software do not meet the three criteria of quick prototyping, open software, and flexible delivery options. Either the prototyping process is laborious, the software cannot work with software from other sources, or the speed or quality of the output is severely constrained. Such packages often fall short because they try to solve too many problems at once. As a result, they offer only rudimentary facilities in some crucial aspects of graphics, open systems, speed, or quality of display. Worse still, their languages are unique and complex. They must be learned. In such a dynamic environment, very few people have the time needed to become proficient.

The reason for this phenomenon is that EIS vendors feel the need to be able to offer a little bit of everything—spreadsheet, analytical support, communications, modeling, graphics, and so on. Like new cars, the packages are loaded with options to attract the customer. Only after the sale does the customer learn how difficult the vehicle is to drive, to maintain, and how often it stalls.

Nevertheless, there are a number of good paths through the software selection maze. Hundreds of EIS directors have taken them. Some bought packaged EIS solutions and others used the software tools they already had. Their experiences, presented in this chapter, will illustrate what capabilities are available and how they meet user needs.

Layers of EIS Software

EIS software is like a layer cake. Each layer of cake is a different function, and the icing is the connective software that holds the layers together. Seen this way, many organizations discover that they already have many of the tools needed to serve major EIS functions. There are four major layers of EIS functions. From the top down, these are:

User interface and delivery: The user interface layer includes the software which gives the executive choices, accepts a selection, and displays detailed data or graphics on the screen and prints it on paper or slides. This layer may also offer analysis, calendaring, and other capabilities.

File repository and communication: The repository and communication layer software stores files of data, reports, and graphs, and is used to update those files. This layer includes communications functions, such as electronic mail, if the data is to be transferred from another system.

Data gathering and manipulation: The data gathering, analysis, and charting layer includes the software that reads information from other systems, aggregates and analyzes it, and converts it into the files of data, reports, and graphs that will be maintained in the repository.

Information sources: The fourth layer of functions consists of the data bases from which an EIS draws its information. This layer includes internal and external data bases, word processing, graphics, spreadsheet, and any other resource that may be needed to provide information to the EIS.

At this point, some readers may wonder why not put an entire EIS system together using a combination of Lotus 1-2-3 or Super-Calc5 or dBase III along with such packages as FOCUS, CA-Tellagraf, IBM's AS, or similar systems.

Go for it! Many people have, and their success rate is certainly no worse, and perhaps a bit better, than that of systems built using other EIS solutions. As with the decision about hardware, it often makes sense to use the data bases, reporting, graphics, and electronic mail systems already installed. If any of these pieces is missing—boardroom-quality graphics, for instance—it can be purchased as, and when, needed. On the other hand, if few of these pieces are currently available, it may be desirable to purchase an EIS software package.

In surveying their software for EIS use, many organizations find that they lack the user interface and delivery system layer. Choice of the delivery system is very important. The correct delivery system will offer rapid set-up and will deliver key information from any of the organization's existing software tools, applications, and data bases. A good user interface and delivery system will also allow an EIS developer to create an effective EIS relying upon software that is already familiar.

Bundle of Joy?

Which is the most effective approach to building an EIS, investing in pre-packaged bundled systems, or adapting and enhancing the software already in use? Which approach will provide the optimum mix of user interface and delivery, repository and communications, data analysis (to calculate trends, variance, and rankings), data display (for making graphics) and, perhaps, a database for storing all the executive data in one place?

In a debate which has generated at least as much heat as it has light, partisans of both courses have mustered convincing arguments. Those who question the wisdom of bundled systems ask why anyone should spend money on a whole new set of EIS tools when they already own software with most of the same capabilities. Further, they ask, why force people to learn a new language for EIS when they already are skilled at using the existing tools?

In the early days of EIS software, there was a simple answer to the above question. It was necessary to buy all the pieces from the same EIS vendor because that was the only way one could obtain the friendly EIS user interface. That interface, using mouse and touchscreen, is central to the appeal of executive information systems. To get it, it used to be necessary to choose from among packages priced at $150,000 to $300,000. Those packages included, along with a friendly interface, analytical tools, graphic tools, and databases whether needed or not.

As an alternative, some self-reliant EIS directors built menu-based systems in the C language, or in a database language. Such efforts often served a valuable function, but the resultant information systems lacked the sizzle and power of a bundled EIS.

In 1988, powerful user interface tools finally became available at prices far below those charged for bundled systems. Packages such as HyperCard, Easel, Cadet, Direct Line, Redimaster, and CA-First Class hit the market in rapid order. Some of the EIS user interface and delivery packages were far more than just tool boxes. The packages support mouse or infrared controller, rapid display of graphics, and access to data and to a wide variety of analytical software.

Currently, potential EIS developers have the following choices: Build a system using available tools, but without a sophisticated delivery system (an open EIS without the sizzle). Build a system using a bundled EIS system purchased from an EIS vendor (a bundled or packaged EIS). Or, build a system using available tools complemented by a purchased executive user interface and delivery system (an open EIS).

Proponents of the packaged software approach, including such firms as Pilot, Execucom, and Comshare, argue that integrating the required pieces can take more time and programming effort than it is worth. These proponents argue that bundled EIS systems can now do virtually all the things that a good EIS needs to do, and that bundled EIS systems free up information services staff by allowing executives to ask ad hoc questions directly, without staff support.

Open EIS proponents make three claims. First, that bundled EIS packages don't have everything an effective executive information system needs, particularly in the area of extensive graphics and formatting capabilities. If bundled systems are so complete, then why are they constantly being revised? Second, open EIS proponents argue that if the organization is already producing many of the reports and graphs desired by the executives, why not use them? Surely it is easier to update and change existing reports because staff is already familiar with the software. Third, an open EIS allows fast and impressive startup, low software acquisition costs, and a gradual learning curve. In short, familiarity breeds facility.

To bundle, or not to bundle? There are examples of success and failure from both approaches. On the whole, we see two reasons for being more sympathetic to the open EIS approach. The first is that, at a minimum, an open EIS allows the system to include graphs and reports which the executives are currently receiving. The coup de grace of many an EIS has been some executive saying, "You mean we spent a hundred grand on a system that won't even give us what we were already getting?"

The second reason to favor an open EIS is that all trends seem to be heading in that direction. As computer power increases, prices continue to fall, and competition reduces the software universe to a few dominant data base, graphics, and analytical packages, more and more systems are being required to work together in mutual tolerance if not harmony. Major actors have recently seen fit to throw their hats into the open EIS ring. IBM announced an open EIS approach, and Comshare is moving to open its system and sell only those components that a client does not already have.

The EIS Delivery System

Whether the EIS is open or packaged, the delivery system will be the most visible component. This remains true even though both the EIS's primary analytical system and the data repository remain on a host computer.

Interviews with more than one hundred experienced EIS directors reveal a number of features which the ideal Macintosh- or PC-based EIS delivery system should offer. First, the software should work on existing personal computer platforms, both Macintosh and IBM-compatibles, without requiring that those platforms be upgraded with beefed-up processors, graphics boards, or monitors.

Second, the ideal delivery system should allow at least partial implementation of a new EIS within a reasonably short time *without* expensive highly-skilled expertise or extensive training programs. Users should be able to interact with the system via mouse, touchscreen, infrared remote, and keyboard, and it should deliver reports and graphs created in any application or analysis program, not just in programs embedded in the bundled EIS software.

Finally, the EIS system should allow users to run other programs from within the EIS, and return to the EIS when finished. This is, to a great extent, the essence of an open EIS. The system offers essentially unlimited expansion capabilities. The system should allow *hot-spots* to be created in reports, graphs, and maps so that users can *drill down*. In this way, users can obtain further information via the reports and graphs even if the original reports did not have such capability built in. In addition to electronic mail support, the ideal EIS delivery system should offer color exception reporting in which certain figures change color based upon pre-defined variance limits.

To date, we have yet to see any single system that offers all of these ideal features. To get them all requires some shopping around to obtain and integrate the best mix of components.

Security—Burglars, Bunglers, & Blown Fuses

In the fall of 1988, if we are to believe what we read in *Newsweek,* NBC television's morning host Bryant Gumbel wrote a stinging review of his co-workers. That review was contained in a private memorandum to Gumbel's executive producer. The memo surfaced early in March of 1989 to a chorus of internal grumbling and national tittering.

How did the highly sensitive personal memorandum leak out? According to *Newsweek* (March 13, 1989) one explanation is that, "The memo began circulating when the network switched computer systems, inadvertently permitting some private files to be read by other users."

But it doesn't take something as dramatic as a system upgrade to compromise an EIS's security. As long as people write their passwords on notes stuck to their personal computers or terminals, security will be an intractable problem. This is doubly true for EIS systems where sensitive data leaks can be disastrous. The level of security your EIS needs depends on the sensitivity of the data it contains, and on the number, distribution, and reliability of system users.

To make an EIS secure, unauthorized access must be made inconvenient. This requires locking the computer when it is not in use. For personal computer-based systems containing sensitive data, this involves locking the office or the computer, or acquiring a personal computer-based security system with keyword sign-on. For host computer-based systems, the only practical approach is the keyword sign-on with forced password changes every few days. Sorry.

Call for Backup

Backup is essential to any important computer system. The more useful the EIS, the more important are effective backup and recovery systems. This rule applies not only to the system as a whole, but to specific applications within the executive information system. For example, if the weekly report of sales by division is delayed until after the executive has had his first cup of coffee, the worst to expect is a few dirty looks. If, on the other hand, all of the principals of a potential merger are attending a noon showdown and the boardroom display blows a fuse, the five-minute delay can mean a shorted-out EIS.

The lesson to be learned is that the EIS developer should keep one hand on the system's pulse, and should monitor the EIS for high-visibility executive presentations, crucial bits of information, and key executive users. In the case of a boardroom meeting like the one described above, the room and equipment should be double-checked the day before. Because few operations can afford to have duplicate, back-up facilities for expensive presentation hardware, where there is no room for error the only answer is redundant displays of different types, such as slides and viewgraphs.

Before an important meeting, all of the key EIS displays should be backed up on 35mm slides, and the projector should be set up in the boardroom. A full-color paper copy of all of the material should be available for each attender, and some sort of dynamic, interactive backup, if only partial, should be in place.

User Training

Developing an EIS requires that two teams be adequately trained—the EIS development team and the executive users. Depending upon how difficult the EIS language is to learn and use, the ideal situation for the EIS director is to have garnered enough resources to hire an expert, full-time, for as long as it takes. Short of this, the EIS director should study the system and be conversant with the language *before* launching an EIS odyssey.

For the executive users, the best EIS training technique is the least visible. The EIS, ideally, should train the user to use it. Any user-friendly system such as an EIS should be designed for the naive user. If an executive is not readily available to test drive the EIS, find a reasonable facsimile. A spouse or best friend (from outside of the office) is a good, and often boundless, source of constructive criticism. When a novice uses an EIS it is often surprising to discover where the main bottlenecks appear.

The Big Five

There are five vendors most likely to be considered for large EIS projects. For large organizations, EIS will span personal computers, midrange computers, and mainframes. Of the five largest vendors, two are hardware vendors, one is a general purpose software vendor, and two are pioneering EIS software vendors.

Because of the early lead these five vendors have taken, it is unlikely that many new, smaller vendors will be able to penetrate the market. On the other hand, one is certainly not obligated to use any of these vendors. An entire EIS can be constructed using whatever software packages provide the necessary functions. In the following chapter is a list of two dozen EIS software packages for personal computers. Earlier in this chapter we mentioned the popular software packages, based on a host computer, which support analysis and graphics.

Pilot

In the early 1980's when EIS was little more than a fond desire, Pilot Executive Software Corporation forged a new product out of a combination of data analysis, graphics, and a colorful, push-button user interface. Pilot's approach ensured consistency of information by maintaining data on the host computer, usually an IBM mainframe or Digital VAX. The data was downloaded on request and graphed on a personal computer.

Given a very responsive host computer, this type of approach offers both high speed and a single common database. As the EIS concept became better known, Pilot's name became synonymous with executive information systems. Pilot also pioneered the use of automated application development tools to allow users to create new applications quickly.

Comshare

Pilot's early lead did not last. Comshare, a major force in the computer time-sharing industry, discovered that selling software was a good way to gain back revenue being lost as time-sharing declined. Comshare developed an EIS product that looked better than Pilot during demonstrations. It used more graphic icons. Because the demonstration was entirely personal computer-based, it was much faster than the Pilot demonstrations. The latter had to use low-speed, dial-up links to get demonstration data.

For two years the two firms fought the EIS architecture war. Pilot stressed the importance of a centralized data repository, while Comshare focused on speed, responsiveness, and open access to reports (but not graphics) produced on other software packages. By 1988, Comshare also began demonstrating a product similar to Pilot's host-based data repository. By arguing that the user could choose either approach with Comshare, while still using its advantage in personal computer-based demonstrations, Comshare passed Pilot in market share.

Comshare got a large credibility boost from IBM in 1988 when Big Blue began marketing Comshare's Commander software. Invariably, these EIS pioneering vendors could not keep the market to themselves for long. Soon, Execucom added an executive information system to its product line, as did Information Resources and a half-dozen other software companies.

Computer Associates

Most EIS vendors offered packaged, or bundled, EIS software that combined graphics, data analysis, and delivery systems. Computer Associates entered the market with an open EIS approach. This approach allowed organizations which were already using spreadsheets, fourth generation languages, decision-support, and graphics software to continue using those packages as part of executive information systems applications.

Computer Associates based its approach on the experience gleaned from seeing its software used in EIS by such clients as Phillips Petroleum, First Chicago, and General Motors. The only thing missing from the firm's in-house software library was a colorful, personal computer-based EIS delivery system.

With a product called CA-First Class, Computer Associates filled this gap with a responsive, pushbutton EIS user interface, delivery, and development system. The firm offered its open EIS concept using software products the client had, and combining them into a customized executive information system. This approach offered organizations the benefits of EIS delivery while keeping their own analytic, reporting, and graphic applications.

Several other software companies, noting the growth of the EIS market, also added executive information delivery systems to their products. Most based their products on the use of packages such as HyperCard from Apple, Redimaster from AIS, or Easel from Interactive Images for these add-ons.

IBM Moves In

IBM's senior executives had two problems that an EIS could help solve. First, computer dollars were becoming scarce and their clients required stronger economic justification for major purchases. Second, the more powerful versions of IBM's new PS/2 line of personal computers were not selling well enough.

IBM originally saw its EIS as a bridge-builder between data processing and the client's top-line executives. In pursuit of this end, IBM first entered into a joint marketing agreement with Comshare, in 1988. It wasn't long, however, before others at IBM saw EIS as a way to stimulate sales of their PS/2 computers. In short order, they built an EIS software package that required PS/2 capabilities and the OS/2 operating system. In addition, this package did not use the Comshare tools.

The IBM OS/2 product, called Executive Decisions, follows the open EIS path, yet it also takes advantage of IBM's Application System (AS) software on the mainframe computers. A demonstration of Executive Decisions has the speed and power to appeal to IBM's clients. IBM's potent marketing forces can be expected to make Executive Decisions a major contender in those organizations that use IBM computers exclusively, and are willing to spring for the new, $10,000 PS/2 workstations for each EIS user.

Digital's Equipment

While this was going on, decision support experts and market planners at Digital Equipment Corporation were looking on with some trepidation. Digital's thrust into the IBM strongholds had been built on the VAX system's ease of use, responsiveness, and connectivity. IBM's new product made many VAX applications look frumpy.

In response, Digital combined several products that worked under DEC Windows and announced the combination as DEC Decisions. Although a bit premature (DEC Windows is even less widely used than IBM's OS/2), Digital's announcement was combined with a provocative business argument which positioned EIS as a component of a larger business intelligence system.

When the EIS definition expands, and most EIS proponents expect that it will, people from all over the organization with all sorts of equipment will demand access. When that time comes, Digital's lead in connectivity will position the firm to benefit considerably.

Information Bank

For further reference, we list below some major EIS software vendors along with their addresses.

Computer Associates (CA-First Class, CA-Stratagem, CA-Tellagraf, CA-Supercalc), 10505 Sorrento Valley Road, San Diego, California 92121 (619) 452-0170.

Comshare (Commander, System W), 3001 South State Street, Ann Arbor, Michigan 48108, (313) 994-4800.

Digital Equipment Corporation (DEC Decisions), contact your local sales office.

Execucom (Executive Edge), 9442 Capital of Texas Highway, Austin, Texas, 78759. (512) 346-4980.

Information Resources (Express), 200 Fifth Avenue, Waltham, Massachusetts (617) 890-1100.

International Business Machines (Executive Decisions, AS), contact your local sales office.

Must Software (Direct Line), 101 Merritt 7, Norwalk, Connecticut 06856 (203) 845-5000.

Pilot Executive Software (Pilot Command Center), 40 Broad Street, Boston, Massachusetts 02109, (671) 380-7035.

Other major EIS vendors offering EIS packages that work on IBM mainframes or Digital VAX computers include:

Booz Allen & Hamilton (Specialize in open systems, some software, custom EIS), 209 Burlington Road, Bedford, Massachusetts, 01730 (671) 225-2225.

Holistic Systems (Holos), 9033 East Easter, Englewood, Colorado 80112 (303) 721-0276.

Metaphor, 1965 Charleston Road, Mountain View, California (415) 961-3600.

Security Pacific Automation (Security Pacific EIS), Los Angeles, California, (213) 345-7107.

9 EIS and Personal Computers: A Declaration of Independence

The size of a computer system does not necessarily determine the sophistication of its applications. The current generation of personal computers can now support some incredibly sophisticated executive information systems. In fact, we appear to be rapidly approaching the point at which the users of personal computers can become overwhelmed by, and lost in, the new capabilities offered by those systems.

Designers of some personal computer-based executive information systems have become so enthralled by the personal computer's capabilities that they forget that the object of the exercise is to convey information. Touchscreens, mice, and color pictographs (such as a dollar sign for financial reports) are becoming the trademark of executive information systems. Charts are being produced in a rainbow of irrelevant colors, and pictographs are being employed just because they're there.

It's one thing to make an EIS look sophisticated. It's another thing altogether when the designer loses track of the mission—to solve a business problem—and sacrifices usefulness for bangles.

If employed wisely, however, the personal computer can play several valuable roles in creating and using an EIS. It is often the delivery vehicle for text, charts, and tables. It can also be a repository for some part of the EIS information, and may even be the platform where the EIS data is analyzed and the graphs are originally created. But its primary role in an EIS is as a tool for involving the executive.

Case study: He was over six feet tall, deep-voiced and gracious, with sculpted silver hair that evidenced both age and success. As chief financial officer for one of America's best-known food companies, he had approved millions of dollars in computer expenditures over the years. Yet he retained a healthy skepticism of the claims of computer people and had avoided having a computer installed at his desk.

One day, he was lured out of his office by the vice presidents of information systems and of planning. They wanted him to see a new financial management system. With skepticism intact, he went to the demonstration.

As he entered the room, he confronted the screen of a personal computer. On the screen were images of eight of the firm's products—one from each of the firm's major product categories. Someone handed him a device that looked like a television remote control. The buttons on the remote control were numbered, as were the product images on the computer screen.

Without hesitation, he pressed one of the buttons.

A report appeared on the screen. Leaning forward, he noticed the report was similar to one of the reports he received regularly (and read rarely). This time, however, the report seemed more alive than when it was buried within a computer printout. Although the information was the same, it was more interesting, and more accessible.

He pressed an arrow key on the remote control. The report moved up one line. He tried some other buttons. They worked. Someone said, "Try the graph." He looked on the remote control and noticed a button marked *G*. He pushed it and at once a graph appeared on the screen where the report had been.

After three minutes of exploration, he handed the remote to the vice president of information systems. "I like it," he said. "When do I get mine?"

The role of the personal computer in captivating the executive comes primarily from three of its capabilities. It is fast, it displays realistic graphic images, and it allows even the beginner to tell it what to do. Personal computers that have all three of these capabilities often serve as the centerpiece of the on-line component of executive information systems. In fact, the personal computer embodies the EIS in the minds of many executive users.

While he was president of General Motors, James MacDonald was asked whether he wanted an executive information system like the one Courtney Jones, the GM treasurer, used. MacDonald responded, "You mean that thing on Jones's credenza?" He was, of course, referring to a personal computer which was connected to a remote Prime minicomputer. Though the personal computer served only as a delivery vehicle for charts and tables created on the Prime, MacDonald saw the entire EIS embodied in the personal computer.

Despite its central image, a personal computer alone is neither an EIS nor very useful to the executive. To serve a business purpose, the personal computer needs the right software, information, and an EIS application. We've covered applications and information in earlier chapters. Here we look at the software that turns a personal computer (IBM, IBM clone, or Macintosh) into a platform for executive information delivery.

Desirable Software Attributes

As dependence on large, centralized mainframes declines and desktop systems expand, the issues encountered with personal computer-based EIS systems will grow in importance. As this book goes to press, there are two dozen different personal computer packages for IBM and Macintosh systems which claim to be executive information systems, or which have been used as principal components in customized EIS systems. We have listed them below and on the next page. Each of the packages can play a role in an effective executive information system. Yet, they are very different from one another. How, then, to evaluate them?

Macintosh Packages for EIS Use

User interface

Package	**Comment**
HyperCard	Free
(Apple Computer)	
Supercard	Costs money, adds color
(Silicon Beach)	

Spreadsheets

Excel	Good graphics & spreadsheet
(Microsoft)	
Wingz	More sizzle than Excel.

Integrated EIS Applications

Executive Workstation	Powerful HyperCard application, comes with consulting.
Probus EIS	Powerful HyperCard application, vendor will customize.
(Decision Technologies)	
HyperCard EIS Cooperative	
(Shared EIS Applications)	

IBM-Compatible PC Packages for EIS Use

User Interfaces with Report/Graphics Delivery

CA-First Class (Computer Associates)	Reports, graphics, drill down, fast applications
Cadet (Cadet Executive Information Systems)	Good network support for report & graphic delivery
Commander (Comshare)	PC delivery & host data access
DirectLine (Must Software International)	Voice, report, graph delivery, note of what executive has seen.
Easel (Interactive Images)	Powerful EIS programm language
Executive Decisions (IBM)	First good reason to buy PS/2—20
Redimaster (American Information Systems)	Popular, low-cost, good graphics, report delivery, best name

Spreadsheets

1-2-3 (Lotus)	The standard.
Quattro	Good user control & graphics.
Supercalc5 (Comp. Assoc.)	Excellent 3-D, menus, graphics

Databases

dBase (Aston Tate)	The standard.
Paradox (Borland)	Very user-friendly.
Q&A (Semantec)	Friendly and powerful.

Graphics

Harvard Graphics (Soft. Pub.)	Widely used & very friendly
Graphwriter (Lotus)	Strong graphics, chartbks.
SuperImage (Comp. Assoc.)	Good for diagrams & maps

Integrated Data Analysis/Graphics/Menu Systems

EIS-Epic (Planning Sciences)	Data analysis
Encore! Plus (Ferox Microsys.)	Reports with drill down.
Express (PC) (Info. Resources)	Graphics, reports, analysis
One-Up (Comshare)	Graphics, reports, analysis
Resolve (Metapraxis)	The earliest.

One way is to ask the people who have already acquired EIS systems, and who create and use EIS applications, what they like or dislike about the systems they have used. Ask them what features they would like to see added to the various systems. When we asked those questions, we were more surprised by what was *not* on the priority list than by what was on the list. Here, in order of decreasing popularity, is the wish list compiled from the responses of seasoned EIS users and developers:

speed;

graphics flexibility;

open EIS architecture;

support for old PCs;

support for Macintosh;

fast applications development;

security;

diagrams, icons, and graphic menus;

and multiple views of data.

Speed

Experienced EIS directors say that new reports must appear in less than two seconds, and new graphs in less than six seconds. Speed is the most important requirement of seasoned EIS directors. Systems that take as little as thirty seconds per display are roundly ridiculed for their molasses-like quality. One woman, describing an early EIS she created for an electric utility company observed, "Our system answered hundreds of questions. All the executives had to do was select an option from a menu. Then the system would take the request, tabulate the data, and display it on their screen. It took about 45 seconds for each display. That was too long. Our executives saw it as unresponsive. All work on the project was halted." On the other hand, if there's no other way to get the information which is critically needed, the executives will probably be willing to wait. . . .

Graphic Flexibility

Flexible graphics allow the individual executive to choose a favorite graphics format. The second biggest frustration, after slow delivery, is inflexible graphics. Here are the words of a woman who has worked for more than a year on an EIS, but cannot seem to produce graphics in a format which will please her users:

"They don't like it. They want the bar charts to have numbers at the top and want dollar signs in front of the numbers. I use an EIS interface development language and have called the developer for help. They act as if I am being picky. It's not picky when your executive users have a simple request and the software can't do it."

Alan Greif, director of the executive information systems practice at Booz, Allen & Hamilton and perhaps the most experienced consultant in government EIS, observes about graphics flexibility, "The executives have been using graphics for a long time. They're used to having a staff that can put whatever they want on a chart and modify it as they desire. They know what they like and what they don't like. Unless the EIS can give them what they want, it may as well give up."

Flexibility in design is not all the graphics requirement that seasoned EIS directors desire. They also want an EIS to be able to deliver charts produced outside of the EIS. Some of the specific software packages mentioned were Harvard Graphics, Freelance Plus, CA-Tellagraf, CA-Disspla, SAS/Graph, ICU, AS, Lotus 1-2-3, SuperCalc5, and SuperImage. There is a strong feeling that existing charts can, and should, be part of the EIS delivery system.

This type of request is not limited to graphics. It is part of a more sophisticated desire to construct the EIS using tools that are already in place, and that is the next item on the list.

Open EIS Architecture

An EIS application developer should not be forced to re-program existing reports into the EIS vendor's language. EIS software should be, must be, able to deliver reports and graphs produced by any popular program. Another dimension of such open architecture is access to other programs while the EIS is running. In other words, experienced EIS directors recognize that no EIS developer can create all the functions an EIS might need, so a good EIS should embrace other programs and make those programs function as a part of the EIS delivery system.

To find out how open a vendor's EIS is, bombard the vendor's representative with the following questions: Can the executive press a button inside the EIS which: Runs dBase and returns a report? Allows drill-down through that dBase report? Displays graphs produced in Harvard Graphics and/or in SAS/Graphics? Sends an SQL query to a server and presents the answer? Searches a very large text file using Word Perfect?

This is a sophisticated demand, both on the part of the requestor and as a requirement for the EIS developer. The developers in our survey who asked for this capability included nearly every EIS application builder who had worked on a system for more than six months. All had encountered one of two problems: Either they had been frustrated by limitations in the EIS software that they could not overcome (remember the woman who could not put numbers on bar graphs) or they had encountered a person in the organization who had developed the charts and tables the executive wanted in the EIS who asked, "Why rewrite the programs in some obscure EIS language nobody knows when I can use existing programs written in a language we all know?" That question is not easy to answer.

Stated simply, experienced EIS developers demand a system that will display any report or any chart produced by any program and run any popular program on their personal computer directly, without forcing the executive to leave the friendly EIS environment. In fact, many are shifting from closed to open systems to avoid unnecessary constraints.

Support for old PCs

Many of the EIS developers in our survey emphasized the need to support old personal computers as well as new ones. In organizations which already have a substantial investment in personal computers, the ability of the EIS to support existing equipment keeps the cost of EIS workstations within prudent limits. Here the developers asked that the EIS allow existing personal computers to serve as delivery systems. Even if the pictures do not look quite as elegant as on newer machines, companies want to give access to the system to as many managers and executive secretaries as practical, as well as to executives on the road. Where the firm already has a substantial investment in personal computer hardware, the developers want the EIS to support the old color graphics adapter and Hercules graphics adapters (common on most personal computers sold during the past five years) as well as the graphics available on newer personal computers.

More than 15 million personal computers do not have enhanced graphics adapter (EGA) or very enhanced graphics adapter (VGA) capabilities. Upgrading the monitors and internal graphics processors from color graphics adapter (CGA) to EGA or VGA costs between $500 and $1,200 for each personal computer. Upgrading just 200 personal computers would cost over $100,000. That is too much for some organizations to swallow for a single application. If the EIS can deliver its information to CGA-equipped machines, it will save that much money and still make the information available to everyone who needs it.

Support Macintosh, too

Although Macintosh computers represent only about ten percent of all business personal computers, there are Macs almost everywhere. At least a few Macintosh systems can be found in upwards of 85 percent of organizations now building executive information systems. Many EIS directors are demanding that their EIS software function equally well on Macintosh systems as on IBM or IBM-compatible personal computers. More on Macintosh systems later in this chapter.

Fast Application Development

Another capability experienced EIS developers look for is fast, automatic application development system. Automated application development systems reduce EIS development and maintenance costs. Developers who cite this requirement are primarily users who want to develop multiple applications and/or have recently lost key staff members who were familiar with the EIS programming language. These developers abhor the helpless feeling they get from being dependent on writing and maintaining programs written in a language that few people know and that requires countless arcane statements to set up even the most basic display screen.

Here is the way a senior technology manager described what he wanted: "I have a whole array of reports and graphs. I would like to start by making those instantly available, in a logical way. Give me something that will let me tell the system what reports and graphs are available and what reports can be accessed from what other reports. Then let the system do the work of laying it out and programming the screens."

That doesn't sound like much of a request, but you would be astounded at how few EIS systems are capable of even such rudimentary information management capabilities. An automated development system, on the other hand, offers a simple way to point to the graphics and reports and their contents automatically. The EIS applications can then deliver those graphics and reports without further delay.

Security

Where systems are actually used, security becomes an increasingly important consideration. Security techniques vary from encryption of data to thwart file thieves to sophisticated retinal pattern recognition systems to ensure that only the right people get to the sensitive data.

The security problem remains largely unsolved at this writing, but must be solved if these executives of tomorrow are to trust their most sensitive information to the EIS system.

Diagrams, Icons, and Graphic Menus

Graphic user interfaces such as diagrams and icons are the most common face of an executive information system. Sometimes they are useful; sometimes they are essential.

For a long time IBM-oriented computer specialists ridiculed the Apple Macintosh computers for their use of ultra-simple symbols and icons. On a Macintosh, for example, to erase a document you use the mouse to point at its symbol and drag the document into the symbol of a trash can. That's it. Now that Microsoft's Windows and IBM's Presentation Manager have arrived, however, the IBM'ers have gotten religion and are fast becoming iconophiles.

In EIS, the icons are useful for building executive confidence that the system is truly easier to use than information systems of the past. Asking for information from an EIS can be simplified by using pictorial menus rather than textual ones. This is not to say that the system needs to use a picture of a letter with a stamp on it to represent electronic mail, or cartoon people to represent personnel. Icons and graphical pointing are necessary, however, to turn maps, diagrams, and charts into dynamic menus. Everyone admits that the executive is bombarded by too much information. The EIS menu should speed and simplify efforts to locate the precise information desired.

The following is offered by an EIS builder for a chemical company: "We want our plant managers to have a system that shows real-time information on the status of each part of their operation. The best interface is a diagram of the process. Parts of the diagram should change color depending on current data. A problem area, for instance, should flash red. Then the system should allow the plant managers to point, using a mouse or their finger, at those items they want. The EIS should instantly display

Repartition Par Sexe	Total	Execution	Maitrise	Cadres
Total				
Prod. Transp. EDF				
Equipment				
Organismes Fonctionnels				
Distribution				

Pictographs, such as those used in the chart above, are not common in executive information system displays. Properly used, however, they can add both interest and clarity. The chart above is adapted from the EIS of Electricite de France in Paris. It displays the relative employment of men and women.

the data or graphs describing the performance of that component. That kind of system would be both familiar and friendly."

For example, one firm uses a graphic menu technique to manage quality. The chairman of the large software company has a quality monitoring system that charts the organization's responsiveness to clients' requests for help. With hundreds of products to monitor, the menu that lets the executives use the system could have been cumbersome. To avoid the clutter, the EIS director simplified the interface by using graphs as menus. The first graph that appears when the executive asks for quality information shows a horizontal bar chart with the product groups ranked in order from most requests to fewest. By pointing to one of the bars, the executive gets another bar chart showing the products in that group. Pointing to one of those bars brings up a line chart showing trends.

A government EIS director building a staff and workload productivity monitoring system has a similar idea: "We need a map, with each city showing up in red, yellow, or green, based on how much trouble it is in. Then we could just point to a city to get more information about its problems."

And a U.S. Navy captain describes how he would like the widely-used *stoplight* charts to come to life: "We use the stoplight charts to show the status of our projects in red, yellow, or green. I would like to point to a status indicator and get the detail rather than being forced to shift back to the menu to select the area I want."

Most of these requests have a similar ring: The graphic menus must be dynamic. If the status changes, they want the color or length of the bar to change, and they want to be able to point to the problem area they want and get the information automatically.

Multiple Views of Data

After starting with an EIS that provides only fixed displays, many experienced EIS directors encounter a growing need to be able to cut the data any way the executives want it. Each executive looks at the organization from a unique vantage point. The EIS should allow straightforward reformatting of various views of the data to meet each executive's needs. At one sales company, for example, the president wanted management displays at the divisional level, sorted simply by cost and by the variance of revenue from the budget. At the same firm, the chief financial officer wanted reports down to the department level, with performance indicators that showed ratios of travel and commissions to head counts. Finally, the financial control manager wanted detailed account-level displays to allow her to explain variances discovered by the other executives.

Perhaps surprisingly, one related capability that few EIS directors mention is executive-level ad hoc data analysis or gaming. Although this type of "what-if" analytical tool was viewed as an important requirement by EIS vendors and novice EIS directors, seasoned EIS managers learn differently. What the vast majority of executives really want is data focused through lenses crafted explicitly for them, to their specifications, with consistent format and content.

Some executives do want to look at data from many angles, but they want each view to have been developed and tested *before* they use it. We've found that executives who want to do their own analysis would prefer a series of buttons that they can push to perform each analysis. They don't often use data manipulation tools such as spreadsheets regardless of how friendly such tools become. These executives worry that they might misuse the spreadsheet or database language, saunter into a meeting carrying the wrong numbers, and look downright foolish.

Off-the-Shelf EIS

The requirements cited above were learned the hard way by experienced EIS directors. Unfortunately, most do not match the capabilities currently available in many popular, off-the-shelf EIS packages. Yet many of our respondents were among the EIS pioneers who acquired off-the-shelf EIS packages. How do they explain this inconsistency?

Expediency is the most common answer. One federal manager acquired a limited EIS just a few months earlier. He explained that the rigors of federal contracting procedures made it necessary to purchase the package even after he had learned of its unacceptable weaknesses.

"I saw the EIS package being used at another agency. It looked good so I showed it to our executives. They liked it. So I started the paperwork. It took nearly a year to get the paper through the contract shop. By the time the money became available, I had learned that the EIS I selected was not going to do the job I wanted. At that point, it was a matter of spend the money on the flawed system or lose it and get nothing at all. So I bought it."

The head of a new EIS search team at a consumer products company made the point even more clearly. First, he explains why he was getting rid of the EIS he had purchased: "We are getting new EIS software because our old package is too slow and because its graphics are not good enough for executive presentations. If the folks who bought the original package had talked to the MIS staff in the first place, we would have told them they were making a mistake. Apparently the executive vice president saw a demonstration and was hooked. He knew the guy who ran the company that developed the EIS package, so he purchased it."

In both of the cases described above, a demonstration triggered the desire to buy. No one analyzed what capabilities were essential for the business problem that the EIS was to help solve. Both organizations soon regretted the purchase.

The software tour we presented earlier in this chapter can help you to avoid following in their footsteps. The bottom line, however, is that there is no substitute for first-hand information from experienced users and from the organization's own executives regarding what's important to *that specific EIS application*. Specific problems. Specific priorities. Specific executives. Specific hardware. And specific staff. Generic software capabilities are great, but EIS systems are like shoes: What's most important is how well they fit the wearer.

Once you compare your needs with the capabilities of EIS software systems, you may find an off-the-shelf system that meets your needs exactly. More likely, however, you will find that off-the-shelf systems fall short of meeting requirements. Then, how does a successful EIS grow? Does each require a unique package?

Home-Grown EIS

There are three paths to a do-it-yourself executive information system: Start from scratch with a programming language such as C, and a single spreadsheet, database, or integrated package. Start with a set of packages each of which does part of the job.

Few would argue that starting from scratch, writing programs in C, is a good idea. Unless you plan to launch a new software company offering your home-grown EIS, you are better advised to use one of the other two approaches. These approaches may seem similar, but they lead in quite different directions.

Using a single spreadsheet or database language can hobble a system in a number of ways. For example, in terms of graphics, whatever charts the database and spreadsheets can produce (and some spreadsheet packages such as Lotus1-2-3 and the new version of SuperCalc5 offer very good charts, indeed) there will be executives who request charts the system cannot produce. If your EIS comes up short too many times, system usage could atrophy.

Similarly, using a spreadsheet program or database language can severely limit automatic application development efforts. Writing Lotus 1-2-3 macros or dBase command files is a job for skilled programmers. Any changes to the application require more skilled programmers and time. Lots of time. Although some such programming will be necessary to create reports for delivery in the EIS, it makes little sense to build the user interface and navigation system in these challenging programming languages. Every change in such a system will be held hostage to the availability of a very skilled programmer.

When it comes to icons and diagrams, database languages and spreadsheets are of no use at all. They're designed for keyboard command and selection, not graphic interaction. You wouldn't try running the Boston Marathon in heavy, wing-tip brogues, would you?

Given the drawbacks of the first two paths, we're left with the approach of integrating the functions of multiple packages under an open EIS delivery software umbrella. This path, finally, leads in the direction of a useful EIS.

On both Macintosh and IBM computers, a solution is emerging that allows Mac and PC users to integrate the functions of other programs through a friendly, icon-based user interface. At present, HyperCard and Supercard are the products of choice for the Macintosh, and Easel, First Class, and Redimaster for the IBM PC.

Using such software, either computer system can be used to deliver charts from programs of your choice, get listings from various other programs, provide fast icon-based interface, allow drill-down applications, and run other programs transparently. As the EIS market matures, these tools and their successors will rise to the top of the heap because they are open and can, therefore, be the preferred delivery system for almost any executive information system application.

Macintosh EIS—Jump to HyperSpace

One out of ten personal computers in large organizations is an Apple Macintosh. One out of fifteen EIS systems uses Macs as executive workstations. From the executive's point of view, Macintosh offers a benefit uncommon on IBM PC-based EIS systems: Every function of the Macintosh-based EIS has the same look and "feel." Just as some executives are very particular about what car they drive, others who are familiar with the Macintosh will settle for nothing else.

Macintosh computers have a cult following. Their supporters are quick to feel sorry for IBM PC users who, from their point of view, are damned to the eternal purgatory of difficult-to-use applications and incompatible, hard-to-learn interfaces. Whereas IBM's image is that of a robust, if awkward, *Big Blue*, the Macintosh symbol is a mouse. This "David versus Goliath" image tends to give Macintosh aficionados an air of righteous superiority. It shows.

Macintosh users caress their mice, point at pop-up and pull-down menus written in clear English, and wax eloquent over their artsy little icons. They're especially proud of the friendly little trash can that lets them discard any number of files without alienating the night cleaning crew.

"Let's see you do that on your PC," they pronounce, scarcely able to restrain a sneer.

Well, truth be known, in many ways the Macintosh lovers are correct. The Macintosh has set a new standard for personal computer operating environments that Microsoft and IBM are spending millions of dollars to emulate. Early Macintosh users found that they could do things quickly with their Macs that were simply inconceivable on an IBM personal computer. For example, desktop publishing and excellent graphic design were available on Macs long before either became available on IBM-compatibles.

Over the half-decade since the Macintosh appeared, however, IBM PC software has caught up and, in some cases, surpassed its Macintosh competition. There are still two areas in which the

Mac is ahead and, in one of them, the PC may take another five years to catch up: compatibility and HyperCard.

The New Compatibility

The first Macintosh advantage is wholesale compatibility among applications. For example, graphics can be created in a charting program, edited and formatted in a drawing program, and then printed using a publishing program all without requiring the user to ask for the graph to be translated. If this doesn't sound like much, think about it for a minute. How long would it take you to do the same functions on your IBM or compatible? What about someone who was not quite as familiar with your system? The Mac does them with a few flicks of a wrist and clicks of a mouse.

The Macintosh has an operating environment in which all applications use a common set of utilities through which they can pass text, data, and graphics. IBM PC applications do not. Even Windows, Microsoft's elegant effort to compete, has not succeeded. Too many Windows users continue to depend on applications that do not, or cannot, take advantage of Windows utilities. As a result, their applications can't communicate smoothly.

The jury is still out on whether OS/2 and IBM's PS/2 computers will allow IBM software to catch up. We suspect that it will be five years, if ever, before such wholesale compatibility among applications is widely available on the IBM-compatible computers which are the bulk of systems available to large organizations.

Such compatibility is important, while not essential, for effective executive information systems. The principal benefit is to the EIS systems builder. The executive won't notice, but the systems builder might get more sleep. Executives using an EIS just push buttons and expect certain actions to happen: a graph will be produced from specified data; a report sorted a new way; a document printed to include text, graphs, and data; and so on. The executive couldn't care less how difficult it was for the developer to create the functions, unless he has to pay the bill.

The HyperCard Revolution

Apple's more powerful EIS advantage is a program, distributed free of charge with all new Macintosh computers, called Hyper-Card. HyperCard is actually two things: a language called HyperTalk and a program that brings the computer to life by reading and acting on the commands in a HyperTalk program file.

Perhaps catering to its customers' near phobia about computers, Apple doesn't like to admit that HyperCard represents, indeed, a powerful programming language. In fact, when you write something in HyperTalk, Apple insists that what you've just written is a stack, not a program. Whatever.

A HyperCard stack looks, on the screen, like a stack of three-by-five cards. Using it has more in common with playing video games than struggling with computer programming language. The user aims the mouse at a button over here and a photograph pops up with information about the pictured employee. Touch an arrow and the report scrolls forward. Far from needing to be a skilled typist and code expert, basically, HyperCard stacks require that the user be able to point.

The same functions are available on IBM-compatible PCs, but their development demands hours or days of effort by a very sophisticated programmer. In HyperTalk, the job is much easier. Hundreds of HyperCard programs have been written to provide the type of push-button systems that are so rare, and dear, on IBM's PC line.

In other words, HyperCard empowers the great mass of computer users to develop interactive applications that are at the heart of most EIS delivery systems. Just as BASIC empowered a generation of new PC users to develop simple programs, so HyperCard allows normal (we consider the techies to be very special) people to develop interactive applications.

Despite these capabilities, HyperCard programming is not the answer for most EIS systems. Remember the price those BASIC programmers paid. Every time they wanted changes in a program, they had to write the changes themselves. Simple BASIC programs were easy, but not very useful. Complex BASIC programs were useful, but not easy to develop. Similarly, when an executive wants a few changes, the HyperTalk programmer goes to work. Early in the process, he finds that HyperTalk doesn't do everything. This requires writing supporting programs in C language. Development and maintenance of those programs can impose a high cost on many organizations, and the systems could fall into disuse.

Several entrepreneurs have leaped into HyperSpace, offering HyperTalk-based EIS development systems. As time passes, we expect HyperCard, or its colorful younger brother SuperCard, to become widely used for Macintosh-based EIS systems, but only as the foundation. A lot of organizations will decide to purchase EIS development programs rather than writing and maintaining the lower-level HyperTalk code.

IBM computer users will also have EIS development programs which, though not written in HyperTalk, still offer the same capabilities as the Mac-based EIS development programs. Thus, HyperCard is unlikely to give Apple a dramatic edge in the EIS marketplace.

Laptop Executives

The image of a traveling executive with a notebook-sized computer containing extracts from an EIS is provocative. The technology is available. The software works. Yet most travelers who lug personal computers with them are doing so not to find information, but to enter information that they discover on the trip.

Portable personal computers are inconvenient. They are too heavy. They take too long to start up, so they are not good for quick information retrieval. And they require too much effort by the executive or secretary to load with the updated information before a trip.

Stated another way, laptop EIS will not be popular until updating is automatic, start-up is instant, and the machine weighs less than two pounds. In other words, in about three years. Even then, laptop EIS will need to overcome a stigma attached to pulling out a PC in the middle of a meeting. The very act can quash discussion almost as if a court recorder walked into the room with a stenographic machine and started transcribing every word.

Because of the many hurdles laptop EIS must overcome, it is far more probable, in large companies, that conference rooms will be equipped with personal computers that have fast communications with computers in other corporate locations all over the world. Those personal computers will then become an integral part of management presentations and can also serve visiting executives as an EIS-away-from-home. Executives who are traveling away from any of their offices will be better served by paper chartbooks than by any on-line system. That's why high quality hard-copy output is so crucial in executive information systems.

10 Magical EIS Tour: Tiptoe Through the Minefield

Building an EIS is a bit like walking through a minefield. You wouldn't want to do either without a map, a guide, or both. In this book we provide a map. Unless you have been involved in the development of an EIS before, we urge you not to proceed without a guide. Locate and interact with, or contract for the services of, someone who has been there before.

This chapter is written for the person who is going to be the EIS director, or who wants to know what to expect if if the opportunity to build an EIS opens up. Building an effective EIS is not just another step in a computer technologist's professional development—it is a giant leap into organization-wide authority, visibility, and politics. Attempting to learn both EIS development and corporate finesse at the same time can be a painfully steep learning curve.

Your first step is to have a pretty good idea of where you're going. If you are going to be comfortable briefing top executives and playing midwife to a beautiful bouncing baby EIS, you're going to need to understand the state of the art of EIS *in your particular industry* sector or organization as well. In other words, this course has some homework.

Information Sources

A first, and perhaps most enjoyable, step is to attend an EIS conference. Good EIS conferences have been available two or three times per year since 1988. These are attended by both experienced EIS developers and novices, and usually include vendor displays and demonstrations of the latest software, systems, and techniques. Many consultants speak to, exhibit at, or haunt the conferences as well. If you need a guide, you'll find one. EIS conferences offer a chance to compare the popular EIS vendors both in conference sessions and in private exhibitions or demonstrations. This can save months of investigation and comparison shopping.

One of the surprising things about the EIS profession is its willingness to share its knowledge. Things are happening so fast that open communications are essential for the experts to stay abreast of the subject. It is extremely illuminating to be present while these experts exchange war stories. Experienced EIS directors know how to solve all types of problems, and their experiences can be very helpful. Finding these people, however, can be a chore. The best place to start is at an EIS conference.

If you want to know how the commercial products differ and how you can build EIS systems using tools you already have, then attend one of the semi-annual conferences sponsored by the EIS Institute in Newton, Massachusetts.

If you have already selected the EIS software and system, then that product's user group meetings offer experienced users who can serve as trusted guides. There are group meetings for users of EIS-related software such as Pilot's Command Center, Comshare's Commander, Interactive Image's Easel, and Computer Associates' CA-First Class, CA-Strategem, and CA-Tellagraf.

In addition to attending an EIS conference or two, subscribe to those periodicals which are most relevant to the EIS field and to EIS applications in your particular industry or organizational sector. The EIS field is changing constantly. New higher-payoff applications are being developed, new display formats proven, new technologies, like voice annotation, tested, and new software and hardware announced.

The best way of keeping abreast of these developments is through published materials. There are many journals, magazines, and newsletters which run useful articles on EIS applications. Back issues can also provide a wealth of insight. We've listed more than a dozen of the most relevant articles and books in a table on the opposite page.

Perhaps the most efficient source of practical information is the *EIS Conference Report*. The conference report is a cooperative newsletter written by EIS directors in industry and government, and edited by Alan Paller, an author of this book. Feature articles provide useful advice and common sense from people who know EIS. Some of the better published sources of EIS information are listed on the facing page.

Good EIS models are the ones from organizations with similar hardware environments and comparable goals. Look specifically for applications in your industry. Call the people involved and begin a dialogue. A half dozen such communications will provide sufficient informative connections.

EIS Reference Materials

Brody, Herb. *Computers Invade the Executive Suite,* High Technology Business, vol. 8, no. 2, Feb. 1988.

Burgess, John. *New Software Gains Ground with Computer-Shy CEOs,* The Washington Post, pages F1, F5, May 17, 1989.

Chartrand, Robert Lee. *Executive Information Systems Are Not a New Thing,* Government Computer News, vol. 7, no. 23, Nov. 7, 1988.

Hoffman, Susan F. *Executive Support Systems: MIS Faces a Dilemma,* Information Week, page 36, Jan. 11, 1988.

It's Executive Management System (EIS), Business Month, vol. 129, page 64, Mar. 1987.

Main, Jeremy. *At Last, Software CEOs Can Use,* Fortune, vol. 119, no. 6, page 77, March 13, 1989.

Martin, James. *DSS Applications Should Shed New Light on a Problem,* PC Week, vol. 6, no. 18, page 48, May 9, 1989.

Martin, James. *DSS Tools Help Build, Amalyze Models to Make Decisions,* PC Week, vol. 6, no. 18, page 48, May 9, 1989.

Martin, James. *EIS Helps Managers Gain Insight into Factors for Success,* PC Week, vol. 6, no. 16, page 54, April 18, 1989.

Mitchell, Russell. *How Top Brass is Taking to the Keyboard at Xerox,* Business Week, no. 3058, page 86, June 27, 1988.

Myers, Edith D. *EIS Provides Critical Details—Without Paper,* Administrative Management (1961), vol. 49, no. 2, page 23, March, 1988.

O'Leary, Megan. *EIS Brings Bottom—Line Decision Makers to the PC,* PC Week, vol. 4, page 51, April 14, 1987.

Paller, Alan. *A Guide to EIS for MIS Directors,* CA-Insight, vol. 2, no. 2, pages 5-7, 1989.

Pappas, Kim. *Executive Info. Systems Help Senoir Execs Manage More Effectively,* PC Week, vol. 5, no. 7, page 16, Feb. 16, 1988.

Pappas, Kim. *Software Gives Executives Competitive Edge,* PC Week, vol. 5, no. 2, page 24, June 14, 1988.

Rivard, Edware, and Kate Kaiser. *The Benefits of Quality IS,* Datamation, vol. 35, no. 2, page 53, Jan. 15, 1989.

Robins, Gary. *Exec Info Systems,* Stores, page 29, May, 1989.

Rockart, John F., and David W. DeLong. *Executive Support Systems: The Emergence of Top Management Computer Use,* Dow Jones-Irwin, Homewood, IL, 280 pages, 1988.

Wallace, Robert G. *An EIS Can Be a Bottom-Line Boon,* Information Week, page 56, Jan. 11, 1988.

Wilkinson, Stephanie. *Changing Corporate Culture: the PC in Executive Ranks,* PC Week, vol. 4, page 53, Sept. 15, 1987.

But what if you don't know who to call? Another potentially valuable source of inside information about comparable EIS applications is the national association representing your trade or industry. Associations often have a special interest group on information processing. Among the officers of that special group is usually someone "in the know" with contacts throughout the industry. A few phone calls could produce the names of four or five people in the industry who have already built EIS systems.

Major EIS Information Sources

CIO Magazine, 5 Speen Street, Framingham, MA, 01701

Communications Week, 600 Community Dr., Manhasset, NY, 11030

Computers in Banking, 2 World Trade Ctr., S. 18, New York, NY, 10048

Computerworld, 375 Cochituate Rd., Framingham, MA, 01701-9172

Data Decisions, P.O. Box 6000, Delran, NJ, 08075

Datamation, 249 West 17th St., New York, NY, 10011

Digital Review, 800 Boylston St., Suite 1390, Boston, MA, 02199

EIS Conference Report, 8300 Greensboro Dr., McLean, VA, 22102

Federal Computer Week, 3110 Fairview Pk. Dr., Falls Ch., VA, 22042

Government Computer News, 8601 Georgia Ave., Suite 300,
          Silver Spring, MD, 20910

Government Executive, 1730 M St. NW, Washington, D.C., 20006

Information Week, 600 Community Dr., Manhasset, NY, 11030

Infoworld, 1060 Marsh Rd., Suite c-200, Menlo Park, CA, 94025

MacUser, 950 Tower Lane, 18th Floor, Foster City, CA, 94404

MacWorld, 501 2nd St., Suite 600, San Francisco, CA 94107

Microbanker, 9-11 N. Newberry St., York, PA, 17401

MIS Week, 7 East 12th St., New York, NY, 10003

PC Magazine, 1 Park Ave., New York, NY 10016

PC Week, 800 Boylston St., Boston, MA, 02199

PC World, 375 Cochituate Rd., Framingham, MA, 01701

Software News, 1950 W. Park Dr., Westboro, MA, 01581

For example, officers of the Pharmaceutical Manufacturers Association's information systems section are an excellent source of information about the companies and people who build EIS in the pharmaceutical industry. With this homework done, you are ready to begin building an executive information system.

Getting Help From Vendors

EIS vendors won't be difficult to find. The minute the word gets out that you're seriously interested in building an executive information system you'll have no peace unless your office telephone number is unlisted. The following are a few time-honored techniques for making the time you spend with the vendors worthwhile.

Like all good salespeople, a good software vendor can be a fountain of war stories about how others in your industry have approached EIS. Useful vendors are those who have first-hand experience with other executive information systems. Ask them to share that experiences, including references, with you.

In talking with the vendors find out specifically which business problems are being solved by executive information systems in your industry. Get more detail than that the EIS improved management information. A fresh coat of paint on the lines in the executive parking lot can improve management information. Find out who saved money from their EIS investments and how much. While the vendor may be cautious about revealing information that may be client-confidential, this reticence may mean that none of their clients has benefitted more than the EIS cost.

As the software competition heats up, the vendors will be forced to provide more and more pre-sales support in order to differentiate their products and services from the competition. Sometimes a vendor will set up a prototype using data that will be necessary to solve your business problem. This prototyping support will cost a little, but provides a lot of service.

Keep a Low Profile

The following is a piece of advice for prospective EIS directors. Now that you're ready to begin front-line development work, the first step is to get one of those note pads with the built-in sticky stuff on the back. Get a small one. In neat letters, write the following on the top piece of paper: *Keep a Low Profile.* Stick the note on the slide-out shelf on your desk or wherever it will often catch your (but nobody else's) attention. You've taken a key step in the right direction. You've reminded yourself to listen attentively and move with caution.

There is a natural excitement that accompanies EIS developments. The experience is akin to parenthood. Everyone wants to show pictures of their infants. Not everyone wants to see them.

EIS directors want to tell the world about what their systems will do. There is nothing wrong with self-promotion when it is promoting a proven success. However, promoting a system before it has proven its value to the organization is unwise. Just because a system *prototype* works *technically* does not guarantee that top management will see it as an unmitigated success.

The pressure to demonstrate an EIS prematurely comes from a variety of sources. Software vendors want to show off their product so that others will buy it. The sponsoring executive wants to demonstrate the EIS in the hope that fellow executives will join in sponsoring the system. Other executives want to see what all the fuss is about and where the EIS money is going. Finally, the people working on the system want instant gratification for their effort and cooperation.

A few years ago, the U.S. General Services Administration attempted to develop an EIS called the ExecuTrac system. That development effort ran into a buzz saw of opposition, and some of the developers learned about premature visibility the hard way. Their conclusion: "The most important thing in EIS is to keep a low profile during the development process."

Problems at the GSA began when a group of very senior managers was not convinced that another information system was warranted. Stonewalled by these senior managers, the EIS developers tried to pressure them into cooperating by making the EIS a public centerpiece. Ultimately, and inevitably, the system was torpedoed by the managers who labeled it a waste of money.

The system was used to dazzle anyone who would watch. Developers showed off the colorful user interfaces with different colored spots corresponding to areas of problematic, marginal, and acceptable performance. They used a mouse to point at and instantly select data. It was stunning. Hundreds of representatives from other federal agencies and outside organizations visited the facility. Articles appeared in magazines portraying the system's developers as harbingers of a new generation of more efficient and effective management.

True as that may have been, the developers of the EIS did not benefit from the praise. The powers within the organization viewed all the hoopla as unreasonable in light of the miniscule benefits from the EIS. It took a new EIS driver and two years of hard work to save the system.

The path toward an operational prototype is full of turns and steps. Target the right business problem and pick the right indicators. Select hardware and software, design display formats, access the right data at the right level, and put all the pieces together. Those steps are covered in some detail in earlier chapters. Some of these steps may present some treacherous footing. If, by chance, you do stumble, it is much better for your ego and your EIS to do so without an audience.

In short, don't show off until there is something worth displaying. And when you do finally succumb to the temptation, only demonstrate what is completed—don't even mention aspects of the system which are either in progress or planned.

Realistic EIS Expectations

The overriding objective during the early EIS phase is to make certain that expectations for the system are no greater than what is *absolutely* certain to be delivered. It is far better to promise a pedestrian information system and deliver a work of art than the other way around.

The EIS-related demonstrations conducted during the early stages of EIS development are most often of vendor-supplied examples from other (real or imaginary) companies. Such demonstrations have a lot of sizzle, and they invariably raise expectations beyond what the first prototype can meet. Vendor demonstrations show features that won't be included or data that is not available, and their sophistication encourages too many potential users to think they are going to get wonderful things out of the system instantly.

A picture is worth a thousand words. If early demonstrations show a system with extensive capabilities—pretty color graphics, interactive capabilities—the audience will be transfixed by the show. Nobody will remember being cautioned that their EIS wouldn't be able to produce such fireworks for quite some time. The demonstration will have set the EIS up for failure by introducing a standard against which anything realistic and deliverable will seem a paltry and disappointing.

Demonstrating someone else's EIS can elicit another type of negative (and undesirable) response. On seeing another firm's data, some of the more narrow-minded folks in the audience can miss the point that their system will be specially tailored to their environment. They may not see what relevance a bank's customer services monitoring system could have to a manufacturing firm's order fulfillment problems.

Finally, displaying another firm's data raises the specter of data security risks in the minds of some of the more paranoid viewers. If they are seeing someone else's data, what's to keep the EIS software vendor from exposing their firm's private files to other prospective customers? In short, premature demonstration raises a lot of potential problems.

The Four Phases of EIS

There are four phases of a successful EIS journey—*planning, prototype* development, *adaptation* of the system, and *expansion* of its use. While these phases can be compressed into a very short time period, as we will explain later, a more common, and realistic, schedule is presented in the following.

Planning

Planning is usually a two-month effort, but it can take as long as nine months for a more ambitious system. Planning normally begins with someone being designated to explore EIS possibilities and ends with the designation of an executive sponsor and the description of one or more target business problems. Not uncommonly, however, the entire planning process is short-circuited because a senior executive becomes the sponsor and identifies the business problems to attack. In such a case, skip to a very rushed prototype stage.

Prototype

Prototype development begins with the agreement on the target problem and sponsoring executive, and ends on the day that the sponsoring executive demonstrates the system to someone else. Prototype development should take one to three months. Longer than that, and the executive sponsor's crucial support may fade.

Developing a prototype is not like pulling a rabbit out of a hat, i.e. a single, isolated event. There is an entire series of small steps that lead to a completed prototype. After taking each step there will usually be something to show to the sponsor. In addition, the sponsor will normally participate directly in planning the following step. The final step in this phase—the step to completed prototype—is surprisingly subtle.

As some wags have said about modern art, the prototype is completed when the sponsor says it is. It is impractical to plan to have a completed prototype on a particular day. The point at which the prototype building stage ends and the EIS modification stage begins is vague, but important.

To decide when to shift gears from building to modifying, listen to the sponsor for clues. If the sponsor says things like, "Why did you put those selections on the main screen?" or "That information is not really useful—maybe it should show sales by client," then the EIS is still firmly in the development phase.

When the system changes from the *EIS Director's* system to the *sponsor's* system, the prototype is complete. If the executive does not begin to claim ownership of the system, there are other hints. The following are a few signs that the EIS has graduated from the prototype phase:

"Let's get the managers in the international division on-line."

"I want to use the system during my directors' meeting at the end of the month."

"Let's change this display to show the refinery prices on the same graph with crude prices. I'm tired of flipping back and forth between graphs."

"When can you have me a display of all the sales offices ranked by expenses per employee?"

Get enough of these comments, and it's EIS liftoff!

Adaptation

Like fitting a good suit, after the prototype has been demonstrated and accepted as valuable, it must be adapted to fit the sponsoring executive. The process of modifying the system is, in essence, the key to creating an extensively used EIS. This generally requires between two and four months, and includes molding the system to the sponsoring executive, altering the data sources as necessary to make them feed the EIS, identifying and implementing the analytical capabilities demanded by the sponsoring executive(s), and providing the types of output and displays that make the EIS information useful to executive clientele.

Requests for these changes come directly from the executives who are actively using the system. If the EIS director is generating all of the ideas for user applications and implementing them in hopes that the executive wants them, the EIS has shifted back to the prototyping phase. It's not smart to mix those two stages with a single executive. Once the executive is on-board, nothing should be added without a specific request from the sponsor. During this phase, the visibility of the EIS director is at its highest. Contacts and relationships developed now will help to define that individual's career path.

The goals of the prototype and adaptation phases of an EIS are to wean the system from the EIS director and make it part of the sponsoring executive's environment. Adapting the EIS to the executive's purposes helps to build the trust in the system that is necessary for it to succeed. At this point the system has yet to develop an independent identity—it has no track record. The sponsor will depend upon the EIS to the extent that he can trust and depend upon it and its director.

The number-one key to a successful EIS is an active, committed sponsor. Such sponsors do not come cheap. Senior executives don't rise to their lofty positions by trusting unproven (to them) people or systems. Like it or not, an EIS will be judged by the track record the director establishes in interactions with the executive during the prototype and adaptation phases. The director must *prove* that the system will perform as desired, and will do it in the sponsor's environment.

In short, the EIS director must display the discretion, judgement and follow-through necessary to become a trusted lieutenant to the sponsoring executive. When an EIS fails to win the executive's trust, it usually meets with premature demise.

Interacting with the executive during the prototype phase has a very important objective: the executive must get comfortable with the EIS. This means training the sponsor to use the system. Generally speaking, executives loathe training. If the system demands training, the executives reason, it will be too difficult to use. In addition, training takes time. Executives don't have a lot of that to spare.

Interactions with the executive should serve as mini training sessions. While the sponsor is advising the EIS director on what he wants *out of* the EIS, the EIS director is training the sponsor to *get into* the EIS in the first place!

For example, Larry Cohan, the U.S. General Services Administration's director of innovative office technology, tells of a case which happened a half decade ago, before the more recent GSA activities discussed elsewhere in this chapter. He had developed an EIS with an impressive array of capabilities. It provided immediate access to a large portion of the GSA's massive database. Using artificial intelligence capabilities, the system could be used to investigate anomalies in GSA, and point out areas and managers in need of attention.

To all appearances the system had proven its worth. For example, it quickly analyzed the operations of GSA's extensive motor pool operations nationwide. When the EIS staff informed top management of the results, the executives identified and removed a particularly ineffective car-pool manager. The system was friendly. If the executive's inquiry required extensive computing, the system's voice synthesizer would politely estimate how long it would take to provide the data. In addition, a simple but delightful algorithm allowed the system to automatically reshuffle its menu to display the most frequently requested information at the top of the menu. Nice system.

Only one flaw—top management wasn't using it.

After the EIS had been in the GSA administrator's office for a number of months, Cohan discovered that the administrator had never once touched it. He complained that the EIS didn't have answers to the questions he wanted to ask. Displaying total faith in the system, Cohan strolled into the administrator's office and challenged the executive to ask a question the system couldn't answer. Within seconds after he asked his first question, the EIS gave the administrator the answer.

The administrator was understandably impressed, but once Cohan left the office he never touched the EIS again. A few months later, it was dismantled. One manager involved in that EIS development was burned so badly that, to this day, he tells anyone who will listen to avoid working with EIS.

"To me," he says in disgust, "EIS is a four-letter word."

What went wrong? The answer is simple. The administrator

never felt comfortable using the executive information system. All the dazzling technology, artificial intelligence, graphics, and icons in the world will be no more than interesting pieces of furniture unless the executive feels as comfortable using the EIS as using a bank money machine. If the executive is hard to reach, the EIS can be given to an assistant or executive secretary. Then, using the EIS simply means asking the assistant a question.

Giving a magnificent EIS to an executive who is not involved in its use is like driving a Ferrari Testarosa into a lake. It won't go very far. And, what a waste.

Interaction with the sponsor is interacting with a person, not a system. A good indicator of how well the EIS development is progressing can be deduced from the following numbers: number of times the EIS developer met with the sponsoring executives, number of specific suggestions the executive contributed, number of times the executive's hands ran the system during these meetings, and number of times the executive used the first person possessive (my, mine, our) to describe the system. If the EIS developer is counting and has not run out of fingers and toes by now, some fences may need mending.

Expansion

If an EIS is to reach take-off speed, at some point the sponsor will start directing the distribution of the system. Expanding the benefits of the EIS is the final phase of institutionalizing the system. While this can be a crucial payoff phase for the organization, it is also the phase during which the EIS director should be looking for new targets of opportunity. In essence, expanding the system means creating prototypes for, and building the trust of, many more executives.

To some EIS directors this process is repetitive and, therefore, not very challenging. At this point, the more technology-oriented EIS director may face a mid-career crisis. A choice must be made: either remain in the security and comfort of technology-oriented projects, or take a leap into executive-level responsibilities. This choice should not be taken lightly—it is usually irreversible. Technology is changing so rapidly that to be out of it for even a short time can make reentry painful, if not impossible. An EIS director who gets this far would be wise to spend a long time looking into a mirror before deciding which path to take.

Finding and Obtaining the Data

The initial prototype will not gain management commitment unless it is showing "live" data. The point of greatest opportunity to excite executive involvement is when the executives immerse themselves in preliminary prototype displays. Executives focus on displays or reports that have real data in them. In fact, a prototype with fabricated data may be worse than no prototype at all because the executive sees it as a waste of time. One of the promises of EIS is that it will save executive time. The prototype contradicts that promise when it wastes the executive's time on fabricated data.

There is a simple secret to getting access to the data—involve others. Despite its potential importance to the organization, an EIS is totally dependent upon the good will and cooperation of disparate parts of the organization, and upon people who may be beyond the control of the sponsoring executive. In other words, an EIS director's success depends upon the kindness of strangers.

To get the data into the EIS prototype from computer systems, or to people's desks, will require the help of other people in the organization. The process of getting that data is complicated by the fact that these people may work in other divisions. To gain access, the EIS director may start at the top or the bottom of the division that owns the data. Starting with the senior manager is the proper procedure, but it may create delays. The EIS director's alternative, which is often faster, is to go outside corporate protocol and find someone lower in the organization to provide computer-readable files. This reminds us of the words of the grand lady of computing, Commodore Grace Hopper, "It is often easier to seek forgiveness than to get permission."

Wherever the quest for data begins, it ultimately will lead to the person who really knows the data bases or programs needed to feed the EIS. At this point, the EIS director should anticipate the following problems.

First, the person who knows the data bases won't understand what the EIS director wants because the two of them are using different words to describe the same data. Often people who are close to the data bases refer to them using names which have little to do with the particular information the EIS needs to get out of them. It will take a good deal of patience and care on the part of the EIS director to avoid getting lost in a Tower of Babel where nobody seems to understand what the other person is saying.

Second, the data will be either at a much lower level of detail than desired to display, or will already be summarized at the wrong level, or both. This is almost always the case, and is a key determinant of how much power the EIS software will need to access, process, and manipulate the available data.

Third, someone will claim that the data needs to be explained *before* being shown to top executives. This often happens when the data in question reflects upon the performance of the source of the data or on any other managers in the organization. In such a case, the data owners will need to understand exactly how the data will be used and exactly who will be responsible for the information reflected in the data. In addition, the EIS itself should be equipped with an "explain" button that delivers the clarifications which the data owners want appended to the data.

Fourth, the programs and methods needed to extract and summarize the data are known by a very few, very busy, people. This is another common condition that can require a clear definition (in writing) of the task at hand. Given such a clear and limited task definition, the superiors of the program experts will usually authorize an amount of time to the task.

Data ownership and access problems are the first real test of an EIS director. They are risky. As Jack Kogan of Arthur Andersen observes, "ownership of data—a simple phrase that people have lost their lives over."

Another EIS professional, Alan Greif of Booz, Allen & Hamilton in Bedford Massachusetts, puts the entire data problem into perspective: "More than 90 percent of our effort in the EIS systems we build goes into finding, processing, and guaranteeing the quality of the data." EIS directors must ultimately overcome the data problems. Some EIS directors need months or years to solve their data problems, while others do it in a few weeks. However, some of the people who try to solve these problems in weeks will live to regret the enemies they make in the process.

There are no easy solutions. There are, however, some techniques that have proven valuable in practice. The first comes from steel magnate Andrew Carnegie. He advised managers to "Be hearty in your approbation and lavish in your praise." Carnegie built an industrial empire upon that advice. For the EIS developer, Carnegie's advice will help to navigate the hazards of data gathering. Show appreciation for every bit of help. Use phone calls and notes, and send letters to the helpers' bosses and copies to the executive the EIS will serve. Remember who your friends are.

We recommend a homespun but effective technique to help gain cooperation of the people who will provide the data. Identify the people who help and whose help is needed. Make them the folks who are in the know with regard to the EIS. Interact with them frequently about the status of the EIS and make it clear that their contributions are appreciated.

The data experts should be fully briefed on why the data is needed and how it will be used. They should understand the role of existing reporting programs to provide the data files that will be read into the EIS. If necessary, the computer-readable copies of reports that they already routinely produce will suffice. In that case, the data from those reports may need to be extracted and retabulated, but that can usually be done more easily than the alternative of asking data suppliers to create new reporting programs.

EIS development is a relatively new challenge; data experts should be welcome to share in the excitement of an important new project. Properly involved, the data experts can be invaluable sources of advice regarding what should be displayed, and the most effective way to display the information. During such discussions, the EIS director should avoid extremely tight deadlines—there will be plenty of need for quick response later.

When the data source provides the first data set, the EIS director should quickly produce a sample display from the prototype and show it to the data source *first*. To adopt a metaphor from the agriculture community, displays are like the rain without which no crop will grow. EIS directors who wait until *all* the data has arrived before they use it can find that their data sources rapidly dry up. When data sources get no feedback, they forget about the project. In addition, the files from the data suppliers will rarely be perfect. It is best to get back to them with additional requests while their work on those files is still fresh in their minds.

If the prototype display is something that will be useful to the data owner, or to the data owner's direct superiors, the effort to keep it updated will not seem as burdensome. Such a demonstration will also reassure the data owner that the EIS is not going to distort information or otherwise reflect badly upon the data owner's operation. If necessary, the data owner can be offered control of the release key that allows data to pass from the control of the owner to the other EIS users. They should be reassured to know that the data doesn't go to others until they approve of the transfer.

If all of this diplomacy seems unnecessary, the EIS director may use the direct approach and demand the information "because it is for the top executives." This may actually produce the data more quickly. Be forewarned, however, that this tactic will extract a great cost at a later date. The price will become clear when the EIS needs support to add more data. One of the marvels of EIS is the multitude of credible excuses data suppliers can conjure up when they don't want to provide the information.

An EIS amateur will be tempted to forceably extract the data from its sources. This can be hazardous to both the EIS and the career path of its director. People in middle management do not like ultimata. They may supply the data, but the EIS director's back will become an inviting target.

At this phase the EIS director should, in every case, be willing to go more than halfway toward the data keepers. If they don't want to provide a flat file (one that has all the data in fixed locations with no extraneous information), but they already have reports which contain the data, an extractor program can ferret the data out of the existing computer-readable report files. If the data owners cannot supply the level of summarization needed, but can supply the data at a lower level of aggregation, the EIS can take the lower level and consolidate it.

The need for powerful selection and aggregation capabilities in a data extractor is a key EIS software requirement.

What About Support Staff?

Creating an EIS demands a wide range of skills. To start, the project needs software expertise in three areas: information analysis software to extract and summarize data, graphics software to create graphical displays, and delivery software to package the EIS for on-line delivery. If the EIS director has expertise in all three areas, wonderful. Not only may it be possible to get along without an extensive EIS software team, but the EIS director should have no trouble getting another job when this system is up and running.

It is always advisable to involve the best people available in the above three areas. An EIS needs extraordinarily skilled and experienced people. Pressures at the beginning are great; what may be a small problem later on is gigantic at the start. If the EIS team is not familiar with the software, they'll blame it for every problem and delay. Should this happen, the EIS director will be caught in the middle between support staff and the software vendor—an uncomfortable position when the sponsor expects results in a matter of days.

Some real wizards will be needed, perhaps not full-time but at least a quarter to one-third time, during prototype development. Sometimes these people exist within the organization. More likely the project will need help from outside consultants. If consultants are used, they should include software experts as well as EIS designers. Their credentials should be very, very carefully certified. At a minimum, these experts should have worked on two other EIS systems using the specific EIS software to be employed.

Identifying the experts needed is relatively easy compared with getting their time. With consultants, the executive sponsor will normally be the source of approval. At this point approval should be for a short-term contract. Two to six months of support should suffice to create the prototype system. It should be clear from the start that additional resources will not be forthcoming until the system has proven worthy of further investment.

One benefit of such a short-term commitment is that it motivates consultants. If they understand that there will be no additional work unless the prototype is successful, their hearts and minds (and wallets) will be in the right place.

Gathering internal staff can be much more difficult than hiring consultants. The required people may be the best and the brightest within the organization. Everyone else wants a piece of their time, and the EIS will probably end up at the bottom of a too-long dance card. Often even the sponsoring executive cannot be of much help because of the other people who have claims on the expert's time.

For in-house staff, one solution which has worked many times is simply to use the experts on an ad hoc basis. A true expert can do several tasks in the time lesser mortals need to do one. Such experts are often motivated by new challenges. They may enjoy the key role they will play in developing the new EIS, and may help out in between, after, and on top of their other work. Given bite-sized challenges, they can often perform little miracles. In other words, if the experts are adequately motivated, they will find a way to work more on the EIS project without incurring the wrath of other project leaders. As time goes on and the EIS proves its worth, the experts will naturally gravitate toward it, with their superior's consent.

Once on-board, the support staff should be assigned to short-duration tasks. The EIS director will need to follow up daily or more often to ensure the schedule. The EIS director should inquire about how long it will be until the next EIS milestone or deliverable, what problems have been encountered, and where additional cooperation is needed. These interactions will help the EIS staff to appreciate, right from the start, that the executive's needs require rapid response and that delays, regardless of excuse, will not be tolerated.

At the same time as the EIS director instills support staff with a sense of impatience, they should also gain a sense of importance. This may be the most important information systems project any of them have worked on. It may solve million-dollar problems or find million-dollar opportunities. They are working at the forefront of executive information. Top executives of the firm are following their progress. Without their finest work on the foundation, the entire system may fall.

Entering the Data

As the EIS director gathers data for the prototype, there is a strong temptation to enter the data manually. It should be resisted. Why not take advantage of this shortcut? Because of where it leads. When the executive looks at the prototype and likes it, the first question will be, "Where did you get the data?" If the data was manually extracted and typed in, the entire EIS has been placed on the level of a clerk-typist's production.

If, on the other hand, the answer is that the data was automatically loaded from existing operational information systems, or from external sources, the EIS jumps a big step ahead. The key word is *automatically.*

Most data entry problems are relatively easy to solve. The EIS vendors will demonstrate solutions when they promote their software packages. Any of those packages can read simple, regular data files created specifically for entry into the EIS. But the system will encounter three much more intractable problems: integrating data from personal computer files into host files, getting data from existing old programs, and getting access to data from external sources.

Let's take them one at a time.

Personal Computer Files

The personal computer has dramatically rearranged traditional concepts of databases. For anyone who started in this industry in the early 1970's, a video screen on an executive's desk meant one of two things: A penchant for meddling in the affairs of the data center or an addiction to the afternoon soaps. Desktop screens were Teletype-like keyboards attached toprinters or rigged to television sets.

How things have changed. Today a briefcase-sized $3,000 personal computer can be upgraded internally to 12 megabytes of random access memory. It can store two dozen or more copies of this entire book, including format, layout, and graphics, on its internal disk.

Gone are the days when operating a computer meant trying to get connected to a central system. This fact can complicate an EIS environment. Getting data from personal computer files into host files and integrating it with other data is sort of like putting the cart before the horse. One normally thinks of data sources as resident in large, centralized systems. Today, however, personal computers have changed the landscape. Much of the data an EIS needs will probably come from personal computer files.

The information stored on personal computers can be accessed in one of two ways. First, the personal computer can print the information to a file. The file can be transferred to the host, to be read in the same way it reads report files from other host computers. Second, if the data is numeric, it can be converted into WKS, the file format used by Lotus 1-2-3 and written by dozens of other personal computer programs. If the current information analysis program cannot write WKS, then the EIS will need to rely on reading the report files. If the EIS is to be entirely contained on personal computers linked by local area networks, then the problem of reading data into the personal computer that will serve as host still exists, but transferring the data merely requires that it be copied.

Old Programs

Getting data from older programs can be a significantly greater challenge. It is typical for a sponsor to hand over a pile of computer listings and explain, "It's all somewhere in the printout—I just can't use it in this format." Again, one way to get the data from those listings is by using the EIS information analysis software to read a file that is an exact duplicate of the printed listing. To do this, ask the responsible computer programmer (the one who makes certain that the old program runs) to save a copy of the output listing on disk.

Reading a large listing file by computer is far more difficult than it appears. The first time it is attempted, expect it to require at least a week, and possibly two or three, to get the data out. The effort will undoubtedly encounter some, if not all, of the following problems: identifiers needed to locate data may not be on the same line as the data itself (the department number may be on the line above several lines of detailed data). Or only a few lines of the report are needed, but the entire report must be read and the unwanted parts discarded. Another frequent surprise is the sudden appearance of error messages printed where the data should be.

Another problem occurs when the programmer who developed the listing varied column widths to fit the size of the numbers on the page. In addition, a column will correspond with one item on one page and an entirely different thing on another. For example, if a new department does not have data for twelve months, a column that normally holds January data may instead hold data from the department's first month of operation. Finally, labels and dates may change locations from page to page. Don't give up. This is all part of the process.

External Sources

Getting data from external sources can be a real flight of fantasy. Generally, external data must be reformatted before being presented to EIS users. That will require either creation of a program that reads and reformats the external data, or re-entry of the data manually. Some organizations opt to retype the data. This path of least resistance is archaic, but functional. Sometimes data can be reformatted using a word processor, especially if the typist is also an analyst whose job includes identifying important patterns and bringing them to the attention of senior executives.

For external data, there is an exception to the rule of never manually retyping data into an EIS. Why the exception? Simple—it works. With data from external sources there are not the same hazards that accompany internal data. In most cases, the external data source is obvious, the update cycle is logical, and manual retyping can save considerable time and money.

Reliance upon manual entry of external data is not limited to shoestring operations. For example, Lockheed's eleven-year-old EIS relies, in part, on manually-edited data. Likewise, the EIS at Phillips Petroleum uses some manually entered external data, as does the system used at the U.S. Space Command headquarters.

Our rule still holds, however. EIS developers should resist manual data entry up to the point where further resistance becomes irrational. Manual data entry can consume too much time and distract the EIS team from far more important activities during the early, formative stages. In any case, the longer one delays entering external data manually, the easier it becomes to do it automatically. The secret is the personal computer.

In the majority of cases where external data must be transferred to a host-based EIS system, a personal computer can perform the task automatically. One strength of the new generation of personal computers is that they can recognize nearly any common data format and translate it, with some effort, to almost any other common data format. With four major personal computer operating systems, and any number of earlier versions of each, advanced new personal computers must be flexible enough to communicate with a broad range of systems—or they won't sell.

The personal computer can access the external host computer, extract (or passively receive) the desired data, and then upload the data to the host EIS system. Personal computers can be programmed to "wake up" at appropriate intervals and call the external data service. Personal computers are persistent; if the connection with the external service cannot be made on the first try, the computer can keep calling until the link is made. A personal computer can also be programmed to transmit a preselected set of inquiries to the external service and retrieve and file the responses. In the hands of more adventurous programmers, the desktop wonder can also reformat data into exactly the format needed for EIS delivery.

None of these steps is easy. Most require a good scripting communications program. The reformatting can be done using a data analysis program such as dBase or even a word processing program such as Microsoft Word or WordPerfect. Very capable spreadsheet programmers can also use advanced spreadsheets such as SuperCalc5 (which also handles text) to do the data reformatting job. Those with less sophisticated programmers will find it effectivesimply to use the personal computer's communications program to capture a file and send the raw data file to the EIS host computer. The host-based EIS information analysis software will take care of the rest.

EIS Displays & Executive Needs

Trying to build an EIS without interacting with the executive sponsor is like marrying a mail-order spouse—by the time you know what you're doing, it's too late to make any important changes. EIS objectives, and the information needs of an individual executive, *cannot be outlined by subordinates.* After all, whose EIS is it?

This confusion occurs most often when a technologist wants to create an EIS and cannot find a committed sponsor, or when a sponsor is found but no sponsoring objective is identified. With no active sponsor, the EIS director can convene meetings with underlings to guess what information the executive should see. But that only leads to a system that is overwhelmed with data and detail, most of which is useless. At the same time, it throws the EIS director into the politics of data without the power to use the politics wisely.

Faced with a system overloaded with information of marginal value, a potential sponsoring executive generally delegates it to an assistant, and promptly forgets about it. At best, the executive may use the system for stock quotations, electronic mail, or news services, and ignore the remainder of data it provides. In any case someone will invariably come along, sooner or later, and ask why so much money was spent for so few results.

If an EIS is to meet the executive's needs, it must do three things: involve the right business focus and the right indicators, employ displays which work for the executive, and adjusts to fit the peculiarities of the business. We covered the first of these—selecting the right business focus—in an earlier chapter. Here we provide insight into how to approach the other two.

Choosing the Displays

There are four basic styles of EIS display: tables of data, text, graphic displays (charts or images), and combinations of the above. Veterans of the battles on the cutting edge of EIS development have learned that some executives like text, others tables, and others graphics. Some *love* multi-color displays; others are color blind. Some like two or three of the styles and a few like all four. It is difficult to know in advance which type of display an executive is going to like. But it sure helps.

What constitutes an effective information display is a very personal matter. Folks with lots of experience in this area swear that the executive's preference for display styles is built into the very structure of the brain. Just as there are *cat* people who cannot stand dogs and *dog* people who cannot tolerate cats, there are executives who thrive on tables and dislike graphics, and vice versa.

For example, while Robert McNamara was head of the World Bank, he made it clear that charts were the presentation style of choice for top management. When his successor took the helm, charts were out. Tables were in. If you're building an EIS for a new executive who wants one "just like the one I had at my last company," you've a real head start. To learn what type of display an executive prefers, the easiest way is to ask.

What display style does an executive prefer? Examine the artwork on the walls. If it's Escher, start with bar charts. If the sponsor has lined the walls with growth curves, there's the answer.

An EIS director can experiment with all practical alternative styles of display before committing to one or another. Experiment on paper, not on-line. Use real data, of course, and use the same data in each of the display formats. It is easy to create many different types of displays—there is no need for perfection. In fact, charts which are obviously drafts often elicit more constructive comments from the executive than finished, full-color, on-line artwork. A good approach is to hand-draw the graphics and use paper output, not video displays, for comparisons.

Collect a number of sample presentation formats (copy some of those used in this book, but use real data) in a loose-leaf binder. Include a red pen or pencil and get the package to the sponsor before a long trip or weekend. Most executives enjoy commenting on different data formats. Make certain to emphasize, however, that they are not grading amateur artwork. The executive is designing the style of display which best conveys key information. Decisions made now can save (or cost) great amounts of time in the future.

Test the first EIS data display by creating four different versions of the same display: a plain numeric table, a graph, a combination of a table and a graph, and a graphic or color-enhanced table. The last uses graphic symbols and colors to highlight key items. Make certain that the same information and level of detail are in each display. Select bar or line charts instead of pie charts when designing graphic displays. For some reason, many people dislike pie charts (regardless of the filling). Show a pie chart and you may get the impression that your executive dislikes graphic presentations. Beware of the knee-jerk choice of the prettiest chart. This is not a beauty contest, it's a communications test.

Once the executive's preferred formats are identified, they should be used. However, the EIS developer should not feel compelled to follow that format slavishly. An EIS with only one style of display will be boring, and some styles of display are inappropriate for some types of data. For instance, charts are essential for tracking patterns or trends. However, if the display is meant to help the executive locate a particular number (telephone number, for instance) then a table is the best choice.

Color should be used for conveying information, *not* for embellishing a display. Color should mean something. If color is used to convey profit and loss, for example, the profits should be green and the losses red. Blue or green should be used when something is going well. Red, which makes the heart beat faster, shouts that something demands immediate attention. If a color is used to identify each major department, the same color should be used for the same department every time.

The consistent use of color can be an effective time-saver. With consistent use of color, the executive will soon be able to read your charts without looking at the legends. Color coding quickly draws attention to key areas and important issues.

Unique problems are posed when dealing with color blind executives. More men than women are color blind, with upwards of seven percent having substantial color perception deficiency. Ask your executive sponsor if he is color blind. If not, design the system for people who can differentiate colors. If the executive is color blind, colors may still be used. But, they should be combined with symbols (arrows, triangles, squares) on specific colors to provide redundant coding that a color blind person can decipher quickly.

Tailoring the System

When buying a handmade suit, there are two points at which careful tailoring is crucial—the first is when the fabric, pattern, and general cut of the suit are selected. Later on, after the tailor has developed a mock up, comes the interactive process of fitting the garment to the precise measurements of the customer.

During the first phase of developing an EIS prototype, general concepts are formed but no serious commitments are made. This is the phase where what the executive really wants, and what the EIS director can deliver, become clear. Creating each successive set of examples for the executive is like selecting the cloth and cut. The second, and more dynamic, phase of tailoring the EIS starts when the executive accepts ownership of the system. A working prototype exists, but it is not yet an EIS. This is when the real work begins.

Demonstrating the prototype will have whetted appetites which need to be fed, quickly. Do not assume that the initial prototype can exist "as is" for more than a few weeks, without major alterations. At this point, the system has not yet earned any laurels on which to rest.

Some EIS directors feel that a prototype should be tested in the executive's office for several months before being tailored to fit the executive. That is like asking a customer to wear a half-finished suit for a few weeks just to get the feel of it. Neither is good for customer relations. Any senior executive worthy of the title will make snap decisions about the usefulness of the system, its data, and its displays. If the executive is forced to continue using a half-baked EIS, its weaknesses will become major frustrations, and the executive will lose interest in the system.

The key question is how long to wait before you ask the executive for criticism, and begin implementing the changes. That depends. Consider General Motors on New York's Fifth Avenue. There, on the 24th floor, the GM treasurer and his staff manage billions in cash and securities and participate in every major financial decision from new models to new acquisitions.

Until 1985, the GM Treasurer was Courtney Jones. Jones had

an EIS built for him in 1980. Over the years, the system was expanded and molded to his needs. When Jones was named Chief Financial Officer of Merrill Lynch, Leon Krain was named as the new GM Treasurer. Shortly thereafter, the EIS director and his development team approached Krain with the idea of his own EIS. His reaction was a characteristic: "Show me." His initial reaction to seeing the system that Jones used was typical. He liked parts of it, didn't like others, and wanted additional information added to the system.

In this case the EIS director set up a rigorous review and update cycle. Every other Friday, for nearly six months, the EIS director met with Krain to show him new capabilities and get his suggestions. Many of Krain's requests led to substantial development efforts. In almost every case, however, the new developments were completed within the two weeks between reviews. In other words, at every EIS review meeting the sponsoring executive was shown that considerable progress had been made since the last meeting.

Today, Krain depends as heavily upon his EIS as Jones did before him. It is his system, not some system thrust upon him by a bunch of technologists. He was able to shape the system to fit his needs.

How often should the EIS director meet with the executive sponsor? Every week or two, or at three- or four-week intervals? That depends on the context. Regardless, an EIS must be tailored to the executive without delay. Executives have short attention spans and even shorter tempers. Why risk either?

Goals change, as do executives. Every executive likes to set a distinctive current agenda, and EIS systems must change often. Some parts of the EIS can survive executive turnover. But beyond a few core indicators, the system will not be appreciated by a new executive unless it is adapted to be responsive, in a flexible and continuing way, to the current agenda and goals of that individual.

The Seven-Day EIS

A long time ago, as the story goes, the Chief Executive in the sky created the Earth and all of its creatures in less than a week. Compared to His job, developing a useful EIS in seven days is a lesser challenge. Compared to just about anything else, the seven-day EIS can be a religious experience.

One-week EIS development is normally required only under extreme conditions. A sudden business problem threatens to disrupt operations. A corporate buyout looms. A major competitor folds, presenting an unexpected opportunity. Under such conditions, the seven-day EIS is possible. It can be done, but it requires a lot of preparation to properly grease the skids to ensure that the EIS will float when it hits the water.

In addition, some organizations are hard to convince that an EIS is worth the investment. In an organization where it is necessary to prove that an EIS can be useful before it gets executive sign-off (the Missouri, or show-me, state of decision-making), the following technique can be used to create a rough and ready EIS prototype in one week.

Before starting, it is very important to prepare the way by arranging the following items in advance. Have the hardware for analysis, graphics, and executive delivery in place and operational. Have software packages for executive delivery, graphic production, data analysis, and reporting installed. Arrange for an EIS director and three helpers (consultants may be a necessity) who are familiar with the graphics, EIS delivery software, database, analyses, and computers.

With this head start, the EIS has a good chance of succeeding. The prospective EIS developer should follow this schedule.

Monday morning: Have a good breakfast and get in the right mindset to succeed.

Monday noon: Meet with the executive sponsor to identify the specific business issue the system will address. In this meeting, look for *specific* direction such as, "Let's target consumer service ratings." Given the tight deadline, there's a good chance the executive has a clear idea of the priority issue the EIS is to address.

Monday afternoon: Meet with the data owners who currently report to the executive on the chosen business issue. Collect sample reports and copies of personal computer files on disk with formats and data definitions. Don't leave without names, formats, and data definitions of mainframe files or personal computer that contain relevant data. Learn the structure of the organizational units for which you will report. Find out which clients are served by which organizational element, which elements are managed by other elements, and so forth. Set up another meeting with the data owners for Thursday morning. Tell them it is to review some first attempts–that ought to raise a few eyebrows.

Monday evening: Study the reports. Look for structure. Much of the time invested in the EIS will focus on data–where to get it, how to store it, and how to format it for review. Selecting a good data design, at the start, will save lots of time later. In this step, look for the *dimensions* of the data. Are there departments and divisions? Are there expense and product categories? Is there monthly, weekly, or daily data? Are there budgets, actuals, and revised forecasts?

By the end of the evening, the goal is to have created a first draft of the data structure for the EIS. Having a data structure means having specified each of the dimensions, and identified the hierarchy of elements within each dimension. For example, three of the departments may form a group which wants data reported at both the department and group levels.

Tuesday morning: With the first cup of coffee, assign the expert in data analysis to create a database with the selected dimensions using the information gleaned from yesterday's meeting with the data owners.

Tuesday morning: Design a preliminary set of displays in both tabular and graphic format. If the executive specified a format, or if the data owners offered formats that effectively monitor the key information, use them. Otherwise, the formats displayed in this book can serve as starting points for a delivery system. Don't forget to list goals or limits on the graphs as well as the actual data. At the end of the morning, assign the graphics and reporting expert the job of getting one or two reports and charts of each style ready by Thursday morning, with drafts by Wednesday noon. Give the graphics expert copies of reports that contain the necessary data with instructions to type the data into the graphics package for these charts. That way it won't be necessary to wait for the database person to provide the links.

Tuesday afternoon: Work with the database expert to get access to the necessary data. Help overcome the inevitable hurdles encountered when trying to read the data. By the end of the evening, there should be the beginning of a database.

Wednesday morning: Work with the expert on the database and sketch out the EIS delivery scheme. Make a list of EIS reports and graphs, and determine the best method of moving from one to another. Specify precisely the choices presented to the executive on each display screen.

Wednesday afternoon: Review the preliminary displays and suggest changes. Resolve the data problems and get some real data from the database into the draft reports.

Thursday morning: Meet with the data owners and show them their data in graphic and tabular format. Ask for suggestions on the format and for ideas about additional data. Promise to show the data owners the first system on Monday morning—before it is shown to the executive!

Thursday afternoon: Have the data and graphics experts make whatever format and data changes are feasible. Monitor their efforts. Work with the delivery system expert to create the first prototype delivery system. At this point, use either real graphic and text files or mock files. Get the structure of the delivery system working. Design icons for functions. Create maps for geographic menus. Create graphic screens for other key choices.

Friday, all day. Work the bugs out.

Weekend: If everything worked right on Friday, relax. Otherwise spend the weekend getting the pieces to work together smoothly.

Monday morning, first thing: Present the very first demonstration of the system to the data owners. Carefully write down every suggested change. Explain that it is their EIS which is being delivered to the executive.

Monday noon: Set up the system in a conference room. The executive's office will, presumedly, be occupied.

Monday afternoon: Show the EIS to the key executive. Record suggestions and changes. Write them down on a pad of paper. The pad is not an affectation. Communications with some executives can be so information-packed that it is easy to forget a key point or two unless it is written down.

After the demonstration, spend five minutes celebrating, and then begin work on the next version of the EIS.

For most environments, the EIS construction process will take longer than a week. Whether these seven days are real or Biblical depends primarily on the pressure you are under, the quality of experts, the state of the data, prior preparation, hardware, and software. Regardless of how long it takes, the steps we just outlined will serve the purpose.

11 Expanding the EIS: Attilla and the Pied Piper

The high pay-off applications of executive information systems are those that use the EIS to make top management's goals, and progress toward those goals, visible throughout the organization. This cannot be done if access to the EIS is limited to a few top managers. Expansion also increases the staying power of an information system. An EIS built for and serving one executive may go away when that executive leaves. A system serving a dozen executives will be much more durable.

Expansion helps an EIS maintain its vitality. There are two basic approaches to this expansion: *conquest* (the Attilla the Hun approach) and *persuasion* (viz the Pied Piper). As you may have gathered from our earlier discussion of the subject, we subscribe to the Pied Piper approach. The scorched earth, conquer-at-any-price technique of expanding an EIS is never pleasant, and seldom successful.

There is one exception to the EIS "expand or die" rule. That exception is an EIS developed for a specific problem, which solves the problem and outgrows its utility. This is the Sweet Success EIS. A good example of a sweet success system was mentioned earlier, in another context. We'll go into more detail here. A few years ago, a major eastern paper company faced a slowing market and skyrocketing interest rates. Their inventory was growing while the carrying costs of that inventory were climbing through the roof. Caught between the jaws of this pincer, profits were deflating—rapidly.

Despite memoranda and personal jawboning from the board chairman to the firm's warehouses and distribution centers, the problem got worse. Inventory stayed high. Carrying costs compounded (literally) the losses.

In response, the chairman turned to his information systems manager and asked for a system to monitor, on a weekly basis, inventory levels in every location. All data was to be displayed graphically, along with the name of the person responsible for that particular location. Displays were delivered to every senior executive every Monday morning.

Within a month, improvement was obvious. Three months

later the firm's inventory control target had been exceeded. The chairman estimates that the executive information system, which cost less than $100,000, saved the firm $2.6 million in interest alone.

The EIS was so successful that it worked itself out of a job. With more than a ten-for-one return on investment, the EIS had more than justified itself. This is our point: The important justification for an EIS is that it will more than pay for itself, in a tangible bottom-line sense, in short order. That justification applies equally to the cost of maintaining the EIS as well as to the expense of developing the system in the first place.

In reality, the process of molding the EIS to the executive never ends. At some point, however, usually four or more months after delivery of the prototype, there is a qualitative change in the EIS director's work. Users are requesting fewer changes to the system, and the changes that are requested are far less expansive. Then, and only then, is the system stable enough to begin spreading the benefits of EIS to other executives in the organization.

In an earlier chapter we discussed that magic moment when an EIS graduates from prototype status, and has been adapted to meet the needs of the sponsoring executive(s). It is ready to be expanded to other objectives, to other parts of the organization, and to other capabilities.

Why Expand?

Given that the existence of the EIS is justified by basic bottom-line calculations, there are two very good reasons to expand the use of the system: to get the right information to all the people who must act on it, and to address additional business problems.

Getting the right information to the right people may, as in the cases of Phillips Petroleum and the GPO we described earlier, be an integral part of the original justification of the EIS. The targets at Phillips were the people making the pricing decisions, and at GPO they were the production staff. Giving EIS data to the people at the top is useful. Giving it to people who can act on it directly can be even more useful. A major goal for a successful EIS is to ensure access by the people who will act on the data contained in the EIS displays, in order to help meet the objective set by the executive.

There are a number of ways to help ensure that this happens. Perhaps the best is for the senior executive to refer to the EIS when talking with middle executives. The goal is to convince middle executives that the system contains the data that the firm will use to measure its (and their) performance. If the data is wrong, then they should fix it, not complain about it. A warm public embrace from the top executive is one of the quickest ways to gain adherents to the EIS system. In addition, if the displays themselves clearly include the names of the people responsible for the data in them, those people will want to review the information carefully, and will become EIS users in the process.

Another way to help ensure the growth of the EIS is to design the system to operate on common, lower-cost workstations so that the cost per new user is minimized. A successful EIS will tend to grow down into the organization of the sponsoring executive. Where the EIS tracks the proper business objectives, lower-level executives will often demand access to the system just to find out what the boss is looking at.

Finally, the *use* of the EIS will grow only to the extent that it is *useful* to the users. For example, the Phillips EIS gave competitive cost and pricing data that helped the field executives make the daily pricing decisions upon which the firm's profitability rested. The GPO system showed each production work group how they were doing relative to overall management goals at a level of detail that allowed them to correct the problems they saw. Another GPO system gave each operating manager instantaneous status reports on every print job to provide adequate warning when one part of the printing facility could expect to receive the output of the previous section's work. At Marine Midland Bank, organizational profitability data is published first on the EIS. Since each executive's monthly bonus is determined by those figures, the EIS is watched closely—Especially around the first of the month.

In all of these cases, marketing and technology were not the keys to getting the EIS used by the operating executives. The system justified itself by being *the best source of the information they needed to do their jobs more productively*.

During EIS expansion, it is wise to remember the story of Tom Sawyer and his task of whitewashing Aunt Sally's fence. By making access to the paint brush look like an exclusive honor, the cunning Sawyer had his peers begging to do the work, and had

them paying for the privilege! If lower-level executives appreciate the importance of the EIS to the sponsoring executive,
chances are that wild horses couldn't keep them away from the
system. Wonderful.

Sears, Roebuck, and Company provides the seminal example
of how an effective EIS system will generate enormous pressures
for its own expansion. Sears developed a system that monitored
96 percent of all store sales every day. The EIS was designed for
the top five people who ran the giant retailer. Within four
months after the system was operational, more than 100 people
were accessing and using the EIS regularly.

What happened? The EIS gave senior managers information
their subordinates did not have. The subordinates saw their authority and credibility being erode—their bosses knew more
about their operations than the managers themselves did. These
managers complained loudly to the information systems people,
and every one of them was senior to the EIS director. It didn't
take long for dozens of other executives to gain access to the system. After all, it was the only way they could review data for which
they were responsible at the same time that it was becoming available to the senior executives.

New Applications for New Executives

Another powerful force pushing EIS beyond the executive suite
at corporate headquarters is the simple fact that there are many
executives, with major responsibilities, that are not among the
five or ten top people in a corporation. For example, General
Motors has many plants. Each plant accounts for a business large
enough to be in competition for the Fortune 500. Doesn't each
of the plants and its executives justify an EIS focused on its own
goals?

Likewise in government agencies. There are literally dozens
of program managers in the Air Force, Navy and Army who run
programs amounting to $100 million per year or more. Why
should they not have an EIS simply because they are not in the
office of the Secretary of Defense? Both they, and we as taxpayers and citizens, can benefit significantly from the savings which
can accrue as a result of the improved information flow and ac-
countability associated with an EIS aimed at helping them meet
their objectives.

Each new executive user is no different from the first executive user. Find a business problem, prototype, prototype again and tailor the system to the executive. The process is easier this time because there are now references—the executives who already rely on the system—and there is an infrastructure. The references get new users. The infrastructure gets the job done.

EIS Infrastructure

The EIS infrastructure is the foundation of experience, hardware, software, and support developed in the first go-around. The quality of the infrastructure will determine how quickly and effectively it can respond to new requests. The showmanship and dazzle of the first EIS will have worn off by this time, and new users' minds will be filled with thoughts like, "What can the system do for me?" Once the elegant user interfaces, colorful icons, graphic displays, and mouse controls have become familiar, the system will be judged entirely on the value of the information, its timeliness, and how responsive it is to requests for changes.

Whether you choose a packaged EIS or an open approach for your initial EIS application, the infrastructure developed to support applications downstream must be based upon open architecture. Without it, the fifth EIS application will be as harrowing as the first. To expand, the EIS will need to import data from dozens of different sources. Text will become increasingly important, whatever its source. You may want to be able to deliver scanned images and combinations of text and images. The EIS may need to support database queries with information drawn, on line, from different host computers, mainframes, minis, and personal computers. The security system will need to reflect the growing importance and sensitivity of the information being delivered.

In other words, the EIS will need all the power of many software tools to ensure that it can meet executive demands stimulated by the initial blush of success. Open EIS designs can be based upon software such as HyperCard on the Apple Macintosh, IBM's Executive Decisions, Interactive Image's Easel, AIS's Redimaster, Computer Associates' First Class, and software from packaged EIS vendors who have seen the "open EIS" light. Or, open systems can be constructed in-house. Whatever approach is chosen, an open EIS will be the software infrastructure that organizations adopt to meet complex demands that cannot be fulfilled by packaged EIS solutions.

In the shift from initial EIS implementation to EIS operation and support, the EIS director's role changes from system builder to coach. Approximately two-thirds of all information systems professionals work outside of traditional data processing departments. Each line department has its own information systems staff who are the right people to build, or guide the construction of, the new EIS applications. They know the information, the executives, and the business problem.

This transforms the EIS director into coach and tool supplier, helping others create additional systems. If you do not want to be the coach, read the section *Top Floor, Please* in Chapter One.

Spreading the Benefits

With the infrastructure in place, the EIS is ready to extend its benefits to other executives within the organization who do not answer to the original EIS sponsor. During this process you will encounter some of the same problems we described earlier when discussing launching the EIS. Again, the rationale should be consistent—the EIS is useful and can save time, money, and personnel resources as long as it is focused on a business problem or opportunity. As long as you can document such benefits for the original sponsor, there should be few problems adding more sponsors to the bandwagon.

The most common error we've seen made during this phase of EIS expansion is the unrestrained and nearly religious zeal with which some EIS directors promote their systems. It is as if they alone have seen the solution to the world's great problems and cannot bear for others not to share their enthusiasm. Our experience shows that executive support is often in inverse proportion to the stridency of the EIS enthusiast. The last thing an executive wants is to give some lunatic computer evangelist a license to run amok through his organization.

Consider that some executives have been burned by computer enthusiasts who sold them an expensive package of promises which, when opened, became a Pandora's box. It is best not to remind them of that painful experience.

When you present your EIS to other potential executive sponsors, remember that it has taken you a great deal of time and expense to adapt the system to your original sponsor. There is no reason under the sun for you to pretend that the executive you're talking to will be any easier to please. It is human nature to assume that what we learn from experience will make the second mountain easier to climb than the first. In actuality, experience doesn't make the mountain any smaller, it just increases your climbing skill and endurance.

For example, recall the experience of the General Motors treasurer discussed earlier. In the GM case, the EIS required several months of adaptation for a new executive even though it had already proven its value for the previous holder of the same job. Incautiously promoting an EIS can create expectations that cannot be met, or cannot be met with available resources. Disappointing senior managers because the EIS cannot give them their data, their way, immediately, is a great way to lose all the status gained in creating the first EIS.

How to get new sponsors without promoting the system? The answer is simple: let the sponsoring executive promote the system. If the EIS is good, the sponsor will promote it because it solves real problems, and *that* makes him look good to his peers. Plus, the sponsor has the credibility to promote the system effectively. The EIS director should stand by, the trusted advisor, ready to counsel the new executives on what they will need to make *their* EIS succeed.

Using this approach gets each new EIS project off to a sound beginning, and gives it a good chance to match or even exceed the success of the original system.

12 EIS Futures: What's Around the Bend?

Executive information systems are still in their childhood and, like children, they are changing with dizzying speed. Both the technological underpinnings and the applications of executive information systems will experience dramatic leaps in the near future. While prognostication isn't safe, there are developments coming on line in the next five years which can already be seen.

Here we present those changes from the nearest term to the longest: value-added EIS, enhanced electronic mail, relevance and urgency indicators, streamlined organizations, standards, voice control, and the information wall.

Value-Added EIS

EIS is already evolving to support hierarchies of users, with value being added at each step. Executives don't want to see just data or text or graphics. They want the context of the data as well. The EIS should not only give them information, but provide the means for determining what that information really means. If the executive wants information about a project, the EIS also should be able to display a photograph of the current status of the project. If the executive sees a problem, the EIS should be able to indicate if anyone else has seen the same problem and, if so, what is being done about it.

EIS technology will support this function by allowing analysts and lower levels of managers to provide annotation to any display. That annotation will be accessible whenever another person views the display. Think of it as the electronic version of the small yellow *Post-It* notes from 3M, and you'll have an idea of how this development will look.

Electronic Mail Images & Voice

Accounting for more than 80 percent of executive use of computers today, electronic mail will evolve rapidly. Voice and images are two key extensions that will appear in the next two years.

Voice annotation of electronic mail messages will bring the mail to life. With this capability, you can answer the electronic mail message you see on the screen simply by picking up a telephone-like handset attached to the computer. Using it will take the same skills as the voice mail systems that are already used by many large organizations.

When you receive a message via voice an icon appears on the EIS screen indicating that a voice message is attached. Lift the handset, press a key , and you will hear the message. Or the message can be conveyed via a loudspeaker in your office.

Images add value to electronic mail by allowing the receiver to see just what the sender is talking about. They are electronic copies of pictures, diagrams, graphics, or anything else that can be put on a piece of paper and fed through a scanner. Cartoons from the *New Yorker* are especially popular.

Images may also be electronic photographs of people or objects that are recorded through a video camera. One might argue that facsimile machines offer all the image mail any office can manage. However, when voice and images are included with electronic mail messages, the executive can look at a screen of data or pictures, add voice comments, and send the entire package to the people who need to act on the information, all in a matter of only a few seconds.

Relevance, Urgency, and Severity

As EIS matures, it will evolve from its current status as a warehouse of nice-to-have information into a trusted source of information that carries urgency and importance. In other words, the system can be expected to interrupt the executive (perhaps via an executive secretary just like the staff members) when an important event occurs. The EIS will ensure that information about a major problem in a plant or the loss of a key employee gets delivered to the executive ASAP. Of course, the decision as to what is important enough will be made by the executives themselves, not by the EIS directors.

Can such a system actually work? It seems so. As long ago as 1983, researchers at Bell Labs had created an operating prototype of a system that monitored research project progress and informed the executives only when a problem occurred that exceeded a set threshold. The researchers found that the executives who experimented with the system learned quickly to mold the system and its thresholds to their personal style. They set the thresholds high so that nothing short of a catastrophe would show up when they went away on vacation. They set the thresholds very low when they were frustrated with subordinates and wanted to look over their shoulders.

Systems have already been built that read the newspaper looking for important developments that would affect specific companies. Although they can understand only a few topics to which they have been previously introduced, they are already remarkable and show great promise.

Using such tools, EIS will begin to evolve to provide genuinely relevant information to key executives, along with a degree of urgency that corresponds to the severity of the problem or the magnitude of the opportunity it discloses.

Adoption of Standards

As mundane as they may seem, standards will contribute mightily to the expansion of services offered by executive information systems. Today, although many standards have been proposed, no standards are dominant in most of the technologies that an EIS depends upon.

As the decade of the nineties unfolds, several standards will begin to become popular in the software offered for EIS. Structured query language (SQL) will become the principal bridge between an EIS data analysis system and a storehouse of data. Document architecture standards, one from IBM, one from Digital Equipment, and perhaps one or two more, will make certain that all documents are created equal and can be stored, retrieved, and displayed regardless of which program made them. This will include voice, graphics, images, data, and text.

Programming standards, especially IBM's systems application architecture (SAA) will help ensure programs developed to work on one computer can also function on others. User interface standards, particularly Windows, the Common User Interface from IBM, the Macintosh interface from Apple, and Motif from the Open Software Foundation will be key.

These standards will be used by software developers in organizations that create and sell EIS software tools. Once they have been adopted by a large number of EIS developers, the standards can help users switch from system to system, application to application, and data source to data source without the hassles that are so common today.

Voice Control

The user interface that most executives want is simple voice control. By far the easiest, most effective, and most pleasurable way to get information is to ask someone for it—especially when the someone reacts professionally and nearly instantly.

Computers can already construct very pleasant and professional voices. When EIS can be talked to, just like a staff member, with all the shortcuts we use when speaking with our co-workers, then we will have technology that the executives will adopt with vigor. With conversational computers becoming more commonplace, the science-fiction movies of the future will need far more advanced tools to impress audiences.

The technology for voice interaction is being developed by two groups of researchers. One group is working on the problem of deciphering continuous voice patterns, and it looks as though they have succeeded remarkably. In fact, typewriters you can talk to will be on the market in two or three years.

The other group is working on deciphering the strings of words in those voice patterns. That's a continuing problem which will be a challenge for decades, but which has enough current solutions to begin the process of building executive information systems that understand what the executive says.

The Information Wall

A few advanced executive offices of the year 2000 are likely to have one wall that is fully electronic. In essence, it will be a large graphic display screen sporting the latest in voice technology. Resolution of the screen will be good enough for reviewing articles from newspapers, engineering drawings, or anything else that can reasonably be printed. A question voiced by an executive such as, "What's going on in Sydney?" will elicit a combination of voice and graphic response that might state, "As you can see from the graphs, our sales office there is well above target, but it is having trouble with the new product lines we gave it." Simultaneously the appropriate graphs will be shown. Then the voice might say, "On the other hand, Melbourne isn't doing as well. Do you want to see their numbers?"

The information wall will also be linked into video conference facilities so that the executive can participate in any meetings that are going on in any similarly equipped conference room. Of course, there will be a video camera in the office under the executive's control.

More Streamlined Organizations

EIS systems begin to defuse one of the most powerful forces in bureaucracies today—the Peter Principle. Through access to more detailed information and advanced communications systems, the recently promoted engineer, for example, will be able to spend some time advising his former comrades about specific design alternatives. Mid-level managers will have a greater degree of vertical involvement in the organization than ever before. This capability builds on the current trend toward worker teams and floor-level problem solving.

EIS will help facilitate organizations with fewer levels of management, as they did in helping Phillips Petroleum trim down to a more profitable weight.

Peter Drucker, America's foremost management guru, looks to a future in which organizations resemble hospitals or orchestras. The executive (hospital administrator or conductor) is more of a facilitator than a boss. EIS is helping organizations live with reduced layers of management by delivering the right information to the field executives who must act for the corporation every day.

In an overly competitive world, as companies trim overhead, they will search for technology that can allow them to work smarter with fewer people. There is much reason for optimism that EIS, built right, can become part of the solution they seek.